D1206183

*Perennials in Island Beds*

# Perennials in Island Beds

*A Selection of the Best Hardy Plants*

ALAN BLOOM

FABER & FABER
3 Queen Square London

*First published in 1977*
*by Faber and Faber Limited*
*3 Queen Square London WC1*
*Printed in Great Britain by*
*W & J Mackay Limited Chatham*
*All rights reserved*

© *1977 by Alan Bloom*

*British Library Cataloguing in Publication Data*

Bloom, Alan
    Perennials in island beds.
    1. Flower gardening   2. Perennials
    I. Title
    635.9'62                    SB434

ISBN 0-571-10892-X

# Contents

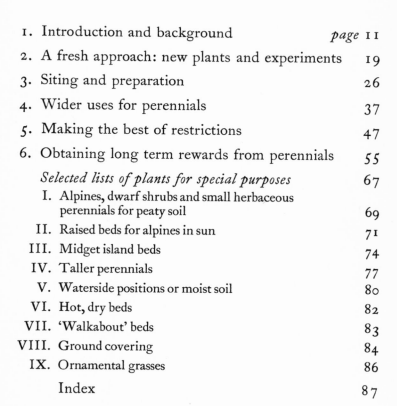

1. Introduction and background                          *page* 11

2. A fresh approach: new plants and experiments          19

3. Siting and preparation                                26

4. Wider uses for perennials                             37

5. Making the best of restrictions                       47

6. Obtaining long term rewards from perennials           55

   *Selected lists of plants for special purposes*       67
   I. Alpines, dwarf shrubs and small herbaceous
      perennials for peaty soil                          69
   II. Raised beds for alpines in sun                    71
   III. Midget island beds                               74
   IV. Taller perennials                                 77
   V. Waterside positions or moist soil                  80
   VI. Hot, dry beds                                     82
   VII. 'Walkabout' beds                                 83
   VIII. Ground covering                                 84
   IX. Ornamental grasses                                86
      Index                                              87

# *Illustrations*

*between pages 48 and 49*

Alpines and conifers on a sloping island bed.

Alpines and conifers bed on the left slope, perennials on the right. Early Summer.

Looking down on an island bed showing grouping for height with the tallest subjects in the centre.

Overall view of beds with the tallest plants in the centre. June.

Restricted use of rock allows a more effective use of plants.

Looking over one island bed to another beyond.

Island beds with background of evergreens.

A stone-built garden shelter and a weeping willow make a background to this island bed.

The rounded end of an island bed showing a spiky but graceful *Cimicifuga*.

The small bed in the centre is flanked by a long bed of alpines, conifers and heathers.

Island beds with conifers as a background to break the uniformity.

Overall view of two island beds taken in early summer.

Overall view of an island bed in late May.

Close-up of terraced shade-plant section with the rare double white *Trillium grandiflorum plenum*. Late spring.

An island bed taken from above and showing dwarf subjects nearest the path.

A view overlooking island beds, taken from the top of the terraced bank.

*Photographs by Michael Warren*

9

# I

## Introduction and Background

VERY LITTLE IS on record as to how hardy perennials came to be used as decorative garden plants. Decorative gardening as we know it now has evolved and like any other modern development bears little resemblance to anything existing previous to a century ago. The introduction into this country of most non-indigenous species is dated from the sixteenth century onwards, but generations passed before the earliest of those of garden value became popular or widely cultivated. This applies, of course, much more to those plants, shrubs and trees which did not readily reproduce from seed, and, as so often applies, the demand was the stimulant for the supply.

Until a century or so ago, only the small minority, possessing the means, scope and interest, went in for decorative gardening at all. Cottage gardens in rural areas have existed for centuries, but the first call on time and space was for edible and medicinal plants. An appreciation of plants purely for beauty's sake could scarcely be shared by many in medieval times, but after the Reformation, with a slowly widening distribution of wealth, references to floral beauty are made in writings of the time—including Shakespeare's. Spenser, too, in 1590, mentions beds and borders of flowers, and no doubt some of these would be from perennial plants. The term 'border' meant the strip beside a path, or that against a man-made boundary, such as a wall. Those to whom flowers appealed sufficiently would naturally plant them in such a strip and in his *Dictionary of Gardening* of 1724 Phillip Miller states that 'gardeners are making borders along the sidewalks for their choicest flowers.' He also recommends that 'where flowers are desired, there may be borders continued around the extent of the lawn, immediately before the planting of shrubs, which, if properly planted with hardy flowers to succeed each other, will afford a more pleasing prospect.'

This advice was in due course taken up and led to the conventional 'herbaceous border', in which 'hardy herbaceous perennials' predominated. As a term, this is as cumbersome as it is inadequate. It makes no allowance for the fact that not all plants are 'herbaceous', i.e. die down in winter dormancy. Kniphofias, heucheras, and many more kinds, retain their foliage over winter. The word 'perennials' is also inadequate because in this sense many hardy bulbs or corms could be included.

It is, however, more important to exclude the word 'herbaceous' if only because it has connotations with the conventional 'herbaceous border', which can no longer claim to be the best means of growing hardy plants. I am well aware that the latter term also lacks adequacy and accuracy, but I am using it because there is no single word (like the German *Stauden*) which denotes the range of subjects recommended in this book. It includes the truly herbaceous plants such as phlox, and delphiniums, together with those that retain their leaves, ornamental grasses, a selection of bulbous, rhizomed or cormed plants, but excludes hardwood shrubs and, of course, annual or monocarpic subjects.

'Herbaceous borders' became conventional, but at

first they themselves were a development from earlier forms. A century of so ago, there were roughly two almost opposite modes of decorative gardening. Borders containing a hodge-podge of perennials and annuals, bulbs, roses and hardwoods appealed most to the 'lower orders' and the yeoman farmer's wife. The 'laid out' garden with its formal and often geometric beds was for the more well-to-do. They tended to follow, on a scale according to the owner's means, the pattern set by the wealthy aristocracy whose vast gardens matched their imposing mansions. The flowers used for the formal beds in such gardens could scarcely be other than formal as well, so the range of bedding plants came into popularity. Uniformity of height, spread and season was necessary and colours could be chosen to form brilliant but formal patterns. Few hardy plants were adaptable for this mode of gardening and, with labour plentiful, it was easier to replant complete beds twice and even three times a year in order to cover the spring, summer and autumn seasons with colourful patterns of flowers.

It was against the rigidity and labour of this form of gardening that two eminent Victorian gardeners rebelled. William Robinson and Gertrude Jekyll were writers as well as expert gardeners. Their approach was inspired by the belief that true beauty could only be fully found and appreciated if flowers were grown more as nature intended. This applied to decorative gardening as a vogue, for most of the great gardens of their century were blatantly man-made, and the area actually devoted to flowers was only fractional. Gardens were designed to show off not the plants they contained, but the designer's skill in the intricacies and extravagances to which formalities of layout could be carried. Such designs had been the fashion for about three centuries, as a mark of wealth or rank. They were anything but an appreciation of natural beauty.

William Robinson was in a good position to be the leader in the revolt against formality. He worked his way up to become founder proprietor of the weekly *Gardening Illustrated*, and his editorials were constantly firing broadsides in pithy language against his pet aversions. During his long reign (he died in 1934 aged ninety-seven) he undoubtedly influenced many people in an age when more than ever before were taking to gardening as a relaxation. Despite his being something of an eccentric and a misogamist, his estate at Gravetye, near East Grinstead, contained wild and woodland gardens as well as an oversize 'cottage' garden full of colour and variety.

Gertrude Jekyll, the doyenne of lady gardeners, was as persuasive and prolific with her pen as William Robinson who, often as not, was abrasive as well. She had a special love for hardy perennials and it was largely as a result of the writings of these two Victorians that the idea of the herbaceous border became a cult. In their day, two other factors counted. One was that a vast amount of new plant material was being sent in by collectors in foreign parts. As always, something new and different stimulated interest and demand from the ever-increasing number of garden owners. This was the second factor. But smaller houses with gardens were being built, as trades people and the professional classes began to increase in wealth and numbers and to move out from hemmed-in town dwellings to the rural fringes.

Such people were more receptive to new ideas in gardening, despite their conformity and strait-laced social attitudes. If they went in for a herbaceous border in the latter part of the Victorian era, it was some proof that they were moderns and they could share the disdain of William Robinson and Miss Jekyll for strict old-fashioned gardening forms. Even if they continued with bedding, for the sake of a colourful display, it was the herbaceous border, with its variety of form and colour capable of being extended from March to October, that provided the real interest and the deeper enjoyment.

The Victorian herbaceous border, according to its advocates, should not be confined to any one class of subject. The basic idea was that of free association within the convenient but confined space of a border—the makings of which almost every garden possessed—of perennials, annuals, bulbs and even a selection of shrubs, including roses. The accent was on freedom, but whilst some examples of mixed borders survive to this day, most gardeners found that 'herbaceous plants' were the most satisfactory. Annuals or non-hardy perennials such as dahlias were all very well as gap-fillers. Bulbs could provide the spring flowers, but they were a nuisance later on; some shrubs took up too much space whilst others, including roses—unless standards were used—could be overhung by the taller perennials and also cause painful maintenance problems.

As the demand for hardy plants grew, so did the supply in both quantity and variety. Specialist nurserymen issued catalogues containing an enticing variety, having searched out species new to the gardening public or taken up hybridizing and breeding improvements in genera already becoming popular. Some staged exhibits at flower shows and these, too, became a draw for the increasingly interested public. Names, such as Thomas Ware, Veitch and Gauntlett, became nationally known by the turn of the century, and by then the Royal Horticultural Society was waking up to realize both its scope and its responsibilities as the fostering authority for plants of all kinds and gardening in all its forms.

However, it was not an exclusively British trait to be actively interested in plants and gardens. The French were breeding new peonies, for example, before the end of the Second Empire, and the Dutch did not confine their skill to bulbs alone. The Germans were also becoming interested in the value of hardy plants, and some Americans were breeding iris as well as bringing into cultivation some of the riches of natural flora of the new lands, including Canada. The demand for hardy plants was snowballing, and so was the supply, and by 1900 the herbaceous border was firmly established as an important garden feature. And despite the fact that to maintain a border in good shape called for rather more labour than its early protagonists claimed, such labour was not difficult to come by and gardeners' wages were pretty low.

During most of the first forty years of this century, at least a score of nurserymen were issuing catalogues in which over 500 species and varieties of hardy plants were listed. Some offered over 1,000, and where they made specialities, a hundred or more of different names could be found under such subjects as iris, phlox, peonies, delphiniums, and michaelmas daisies. This could be called the heyday of the herbaceous border. Looking back, I can see now that when I began from scratch in 1926, with youthful ambitions to become a leading specialist in hardy plants, I should have failed had I persisted in imagining I could succeed as a retail nurseryman in the face of such competition. In switching over to wholesale only production in 1934, my business managed to survive, whereas during the next thirty years nearly all those who stuck to retail faded out for one reason or another. The underlying reason, which also deterred others from setting up in the post-war years, was lack of demand. Retailers who no longer found hardy plants remunerative to grow for sale themselves came to me as a wholesaler with a wide range at prices which gave them a more worthwhile margin.

All this is not irrelevant. It is put in to illustrate, from the production angle, the slow rise and sudden decline in popularity of hardy plants, with 1939 as the year in which so many disruptions began. From the garden-owners' angle it marked the end of an era of cheap and abundant labour, and brought about an imperative need for labour-saving on non-essentials.

No form of gardening is entirely trouble-free. Lawns need mowing, trees and shrubs need pruning and so on. But the conventional herbaceous border needed, next to rock-gardens, far more attention than most people could give, if they were not to become quickly bedraggled and unkempt. A shrubbery could be left more or less to look after itself for a season except for easily killed surface weeds. But for a herbaceous border or rock garden a season's neglect would be wellnigh ruinous, and many an attractive garden was, after 1939, spoiled because of neglect, which was often unavoidable at a time when priorities came in for drastic rearrangements. Many a border strip, with its backing wall, fence or hedge, which in 1939 was a colourful herbaceous border had become a shrubbery ten years later.

At about that time, when attempting to re-establish my stocks of hardy plants after they had been decimated by wartime needs, I fell to wondering about the her-baceous border—the means by which most people grew the plants which I was in business to produce. There came a recurring thought that although I could not then imagine any means other than the conventional border with a backing, gardeners in the post-war inflationary period with its scarcity of labour could not be blamed if they shied away from the succession of chores which borders demanded. There was a reasonably good demand for plants at that time, but this could be put down to the release from wartime tensions and restrictions. It was conceivable that hardy plants would soon lose popularity because the usual means of growing them was time-taking and troublesome. As a producer, but one with a love for plants that went much beyond commercial considerations, it was up to me to do some hard thinking, and maybe make another decision, such as I had done in 1934 when opting to grow for wholesale only.

# 2

## *A Fresh Approach: New Plants and Experiments*

THE FIRST GLIMPSE of a new approach came to me one evening in early June 1951. The spring rush in the nursery had just eased, and so had overnight rain and wind. My border near the house had suffered badly from that wind, and caused me to wish once more that I had made time to do the staking before plants had grown so tall. It should have been done three or four weeks before, but other jobs had taken first place. Almost every year it was the same and all the borders in other gardens I had owned had, over the years, brought trouble if May staking had been delayed. These borders had all been on conventional lines, backed by a fence, hedge or wall, as strips varying from 6 to 12 ft. (180–360 cm.) wide, with varying southerly aspects. In them I grew many of my favourites, from 6 ft. (180 cm.) delphiniums down to 6 in. (15 cm.) campanulas at the front. The latter needed no supports, but almost everything did that grew over 2 ft. (60 cm.) tall. In open nursery rows, stems did not grow so tall, and no staking was ever practised because the plants were being grown for sale, not for the flowers.

It occurred to me then that if plants grew with the protection of a backing, this could encourage stem weakness. The effect of being buffeted by wind and rain in the open nursery fields, through the early stages of growth, might well be to produce plants with stronger, shorter stems, which would therefore be less liable to flop than those massed in a backed border. Massing had always been the criterion for the best effect in a conventional border, so that no bare patches or gaps spoiled the pattern of greenery and colourful flowers. But now I began to see that if the backing wall or whatever induced over-tall, lanky stems, preventing the free circulation of air, the taller kinds tended to lean forwards away from the wall, often to the detriment of lowlier kinds in front, so that they too were denied both light and air.

These observations pointed strongly to the baneful effect of a backing, if one wished to grow hardy plants which in nature enjoyed open positions. The herbaceous border was a concept aiming towards naturalness in decorative gardening, but it did not go far enough. The wall, fence, or hungry hedge at the rear, the cramming of plants in varying heights, down to some kind of edging, was still restrictive, causing growth weakness as well as making access for maintenance difficult. And it did very little towards allowing plants to grow naturally especially if, by way of edging, box-hedging in which slugs and snails could find harbourage, was used in front.

I had seen examples of herbaceous borders on the grand scale. Some were double, with a central path, but otherwise the pattern was invariable, for to each there was a backing. One such border I had seen in a large semi-public garden, just after being staked—at the correct time in early May—and to me that vast array of pea-sticks was an eyesore, completely spoiling the effect of early flowering subjects. It made me shudder, because staking was a task I heartily disliked. Because it was such a tiresome nuisance from start to finish, I often skimped it, believing it to be only slightly the lesser of two evils. I was now convinced that there must be a better way of growing hardy plants than in the conventional backed border, and if anyone had the necessary incentive to find such a way, it should be me, for hardy plants were also my bread and butter.

The previous occupants of Bressingham Hall were not garden-minded. They had abandoned a large lawn in front of the house several weeks before I took possession at Michaelmas and for three years now it had remained an apology for a lawn, whilst other more vital things needed attention. But now I saw it as an ideal place for some experiments, based on the general notion that to obtain best results from hardy plants they should be in beds that allowed them to grow as naturally as possible. If light and air, adequate spacing and rational grouping were vital factors, the way to find proof would be to carve out a series of beds in the big lawn in such a way that all-round access as well as good visibility would be achieved. Each bed would be an island in the greensward. If, as was quite likely, someone else had previously tried out island beds, I had not heard of it. What struck me, as I planned and planted these new beds, was the fact that I had been so hidebound to convention myself for so long without the idea occurring to me before. As an alternative—the only alternative I could think of—it appeared now as so obvious a solution that I was convinced it would succeed. It would take two seasons' growth to prove beyond all doubt that much less staking would be needed. This factor would have to be the platform on which any advocacy I could make in favour of island beds must be made, and knowing that full growth could not take place until the second summer I had to be patient.

Meantime, there was scope for secondary experiments. These included the use of dwarf kinds in groups around the edges, which are mostly classed as rock garden plants. The tallest kinds naturally came in for groups towards the centre of each bed with far longer margins to be planted than in the conventional one-sided border and a larger variety of dwarf subjects was needed. This suited me because I also grew alpine and rock garden plants commercially and, as with all I grew in the nursery, I could pick and choose at will and at no cost, in the knowledge that whatever I planted in the new beds could come in for stock reserves, as cuttings, seed or divisions. I could also follow my fancy in siting groups of different kinds, with different habits, foliage, colour and time of flowering, making foils and focal points, whilst still keeping to the basic principles of reducing time and trouble of maintenance.

Some of the first experimental plantings proved to be errors of judgement in the first season. But these were only minor—such as the use of aubrieta and mossy saxifrages as frontal groups, or the switching of a few other groups into more pleasing or appropriate positions. The general effect in that first summer came well up to expectations, and the proof I needed came in the second, the summer of 1953, which was damp enough to produce maximum growth. Early delphiniums had needed staking in 1952 and now with full growth very little else besides showed signs of weakness. As a proportion it was well under 10 per cent of subjects which, in a one-sided border, would have needed support. It was of no consequence whether or not these beds were unique, but the enthusiasm for them and the stimulation they provided made me wish to proclaim the good news far and wide. They also made me yearn to grow in the widest possible variety to include shade and moisture-loving kinds, along with many other species of hardy plants which could be acquired by swopping and which till now existed only as names to me.

The scope was there. Beyond the new beds was a shelter bed of evergreens. Beyond that was a 6-acre (2.43 ha.) meadow set with specimen trees, having a dip, known as the Dell, where the moist loamy soil was cool from shading oak trees. It was another three or four years before the dream of making more island beds in the Dell meadow began to take shape. Till now, the few woodland plants I had grown were in the nursery, under artificial shade, with irrigation, mostly in pots and all for sale to the trade. But now I could think of growing them under natural conditions, for their own sake, as a plantsman should.

I have already written of how an additional 5 acres (2.02 ha.) was given over to island beds and how it came to hold about 5,000 species and varieties of plants. I have learnt something about plants in the twenty years since my first experimental island beds were made, because most of my time since then has been spent in observing them in the process of planting, maintenance and propagation. To take the edge off my successes with plants have come some baffling failures, but all in all the experience has not only encouraged me to speak out in favour of hardy plants in general and island beds in particular, but as a nurseryman too, I have been able to distribute several worthwhile species rescued from obscurity and to introduce new varieties raised here, because the scope and opportunity of doing so was on my doorstep.

Being placed in so fortunate a position, it quickly became a habit not only to be on the constant look-out for kinds which would widen the range in my garden, but to assess their value as good garden plants by growing them under fairly natural conditions. Every kind has its limits imposed by nature, of adaptability to varying conditions of sun, or shade, dryness and moisture, as well as differing soils and climate. Having many such variables at Bressingham, set in the middle of East Anglia where the climate is often quite harsh, has enabled me to judge more fairly such questions as reliability and adaptability. Some conclusions reached here came by trial and error. I have discovered several preconceived notions to be faulty, but in general the conclusion reached is that the majority of hardy plants have a wider range of adaptability than I expected.

It follows that the closer one can get to providing conditions of soil and situation to those which are natural for any given subject, the better the results. This means that, ideally, the whole range should be placed in categories. It would be folly, for example, to plant a shade and moisture lover in a dry, sunny bed along with other kinds that preferred dry, sunny conditions. And because conditions in gardens vary greatly according to soil, climate, aspect and environment, a selection should be made of kinds best adapted or endowed for existing conditions— unless one is prepared to go to the trouble and expense of changing the conditions to suit. Despite what I have said about the adaptability of hardy plants, they do have their limits and these should be known before a selection is made for any given site or situation.

For easy reference, the perennial plants recommended at the end of the book are placed in categories. Although I am utterly convinced that the island bed is by far the best means of growing the widest range of good subjects, there may be some readers who, for one reason or another, will decide they have no place or space for one but it is hoped they will still find useful recommendations in the various lists. The more adaptable hardy plants will appear in more than one list; many less adaptable and less garden-worthy do not appear at all, because the emphasis is placed firmly on the best. Readers will be able to make a selection which will prove the value of hardy plants as an essential, reliable and wholly satisfying aspect of decorative gardening.

# 3
## Siting and Preparation

———◦✦◦———

THIS CHAPTER BEGINS with the assumption that some readers will have been, at least in theory, won over to the island bed concept. Later on, I will do what I can in advising how to make the best use of a conventional one-sided border, for those who have little or no option.

The site most likely to be chosen in many gardens with rectangular boundaries would be more or less as a centre-piece in a lawn. In this case, its shape should be formal—oval, round, square or oblong. Its size would depend on other factors, including one's purse, in the knowledge that four or five good nursery plants would be needed on average per square yard.

Wherever one decides to place an island bed, with all-round access, its position as far as view from the house, or as a focal point, should be considered. It can, for example, be so arranged that the tallest subjects are almost, but not quite, at what would be the rear, taking the view into account. Access and view are not necessarily combined factors, but merely complementary. Rear access to a bed arranged for a more one-sided view would be a convenience and a possible means of growing spring-flowering or shade-loving dwarf plants in an otherwise open position, with tall kinds providing some shade in summer.

An island bed can be as varied in size or area as the

range of plants it contains. The larger it is—especially in width—the greater the range of height, but a midget bed of, say, 6 ft. (180 cm.) in width should exclude any subject growing more than about 3 ft. (90 cm.) tall to obtain a pleasing proportion, with much dwarfer kinds around the perimeter.

Such matters as the selection of plants according to aspect, type of soil and the shade or moisture factor must come after a decision has been taken as to the best site from a decorative viewpoint. A far greater selection can be made from subjects preferring an open, mainly sunny situation, and with this in mind the next step is preparation. If the bed is to replace some lawn space, or ground not already in cultivation, thorough digging will be necessary. A heavy clay-based soil may need draining first, and so long as a slope or outfall can be found, the insertion of land drain tiles or pipes 2 ft. (60 cm.) deep is not a difficult task. The addition of coarse sand, peat or well-spent ashes will greatly improve the texture and workability of heavy clay soil, just as peat or other humus forms will enrich shallow, sandy, gravelly or chalky soils. Double digging is seldom advisable with these, but where heavy or panned soil exists the second spit turned up and loosened, adding sand or humus, will improve drainage as well as fertility. Never bring subsoil on to the surface if it can be avoided.

Perennial weeds must be forked out or killed and this is easier to accomplish in summer than in winter, whether a fork or a chemical spray is used. Where green turf is not wanted elsewhere, it should be chopped up into small pieces and then buried with the preparative digging. Large lumps of turf will shrink when buried and this, through lack of consolidation, could be harmful to plant growth. Wireworm in turf can also cause harm, but a dusting of a killing agent will prove a good insurance against these pests, which are often unsuspected at the time of digging. It may be necessary to mention that heavy soil is best dug in autumn to allow winter weathering in readiness for planting in spring, whereas light soils which do not turn up in clods can be prepared at almost any time. Treading over wet soil should be avoided if in any way possible.

This is the point at which to recapitulate on the main principles of island beds for hardy plants. The first is that the absence of a background hedge, wall or fence allows a better circulation of air, thus promoting stronger, more erect but less lanky stem growth. This will obviate a large amount of staking, as well as making access for weeding, etc. much easier, and the general appearance in summer is greatly enhanced. There are, however, certain secondary factors that will contribute to full success and enjoyment. Just as with ingredients for a cake recipe, it is how the ingredients are proportioned, mixed and baked that makes all the difference.

The ingredients in this case are a selection of colourful, reliable, hardy plants, suitable or adaptable to the soil one has and the position one has chosen, and a bed in which to plant them. Ample variety exists to meet all the variables in a garden, but because the plants themselves vary in height, season of flower and habit, the placing of different kinds in appropriate positions within the bed is of vital importance. If view as well as access count for anything at all, the tallest kinds should be placed in the centre part of an island bed and heights should be graded down to the dwarfest around the edges. The only exception to this would be where a more one-sided view is preferred, to see as much of the range as possible from, say, the house without having to walk round the bed. In this event, the tallest would be closer to the far side, as already mentioned. In all cases, grouping cannot be too strongly recommended. It would be possible, of course, for those with very limited space and means to have a small island bed planted with one plant of each kind and no one would blame those who did this either because of necessity, or simply because they craved maximum variety.

For effect, in both form and colour, groups should be of not less than three of a kind. For large beds a dozen of a kind would not be too many. But personal preferences must have scope, and ample scope exists not only for those to whom a wide variety and continuity appeal, but for those who wish to have seasonal displays for any period between March and October. Preferences may occur for certain colours, or for plants with as much or more appeal in their foliage as in their flowers, or as a source of material for flower arrangements. No other section of decorative plants offers so wide a scope in providing enormous variety on a long-term basis and at a modest cost which includes the plants themselves and their maintenance.

Hardy plants in this context include both the truly herbaceous kinds and those that retain their foliage over winter. They do not include certain shrubs which can be cut back annually to flower on young wood, nor any hardwood subjects such as lavender or hyssop, which, however, could be included if one wished in an assortment that would not be out of place in a frontal group of an island bed. I am including certain bulbous or cormrooted plants which are fully complementary as well as being reliable, but excluding bulbs which have only a brief season above ground and die back to leave a bare patch for long afterwards. For frontal groups, especially in small island beds, some kinds need to be only a few inches tall. What are classed as rock garden plants are in the main just dwarf hardy plants and if they are adaptable, and can play their part in the general scheme, then there is every reason for using them. I have used them for years as frontal groups to beds containing quite tall subjects farther in, and would not consider dispensing with them just because they are considered to be rock garden plants.

One big advantage of grouping, apart from providing a greater display, is that of spacing. Three or more plants of a kind can be set somewhat close together, thus growing more effectively, because more space between the group and its neighbours allows for natural expansion and better access for maintenance. A further advantage lies in being able to avoid flatness or regimentation. Although form, habit, colour and flowering time are infinitely variable, hardy plants can in a general way be divided into the spiky or feathery kinds and those which flower more or less at the same level—such as michaelmas daisies and heleniums. Groups can be so arranged that their flowering habits are interspersed for the most pleasing effect, and opportunities can be made for a group or clump to be used as an outstanding or focal point because it is more effective in some isolation. Kniphofias are especially useful for this form of pattern planning, as are some of the ornamental grasses.

Any thoughts on planning lead to questions of spacing, both between groups and member plants of a group. In the knowledge that different kinds have several different rates of growth and spread, it means that planning and spacing must allow for this. It would be a mistake to plant everything at a uniform distance apart, because the differences in spread, whether of annual above-ground growth or of the plants themselves, could cause trouble. To plan a bed with equal spacings throughout would lead to harmful competition. My recommendations in the selected lists exclude over-rampant kinds, because some can become invasive, if not weedy. Some thought to segregation would be advisable for those who wish to include kinds with invasive tendencies, for it would be asking for trouble to have as neighbours to a slow grower others that grow three or four times as fast in outward spread.

Planning a bed is not so formidable a task as one unfamiliar with plants might think and it is, in fact, an interesting and informative exercise for anyone with leanings towards hardy plants. Having reached a decision on where to place a bed and the space it should occupy, as well as selecting a basic list of kinds one would like to grow, a pencil, rubber and a sheet of graph paper are the only requisites, along with such a book as this for guidance. First number the expected group spaces to be filled and, to save writing in names on the plan, use the group number against the name of the plant selected from your list to occupy that space. It matters not whether you begin by filling in from the tallest in the centre or from the dwarfest on the perimeter, for as the job proceeds all the factors of height, colour, habit and time of flowering can be taken into account for blending or contrasting, not forgetting the importance of height in relation to the overall width of the bed.

This needs a little more explanation. To ensure a pleasing overall appearance, and to avoid incongruity, heights should be restricted where ample width is not available. There are kinds which will tower 6 ft. (180 cm.) or more without the necessity of staking, but these need depth, so that heights range down fairly gradually.

If a bed is only 6–8 ft. (180–240 cm.) or more wide, a six-footer would be out of place, spoiling the effect, if not the growth, of something a foot or two next to it. A safe guide is to exclude kinds which attain heights in excess of half the width of the bed. If it is 8 ft. (240 cm.) wide, have nothing taller than 4 ft. (120 cm.) or thereabouts, bearing in mind that spiky flowered kinds even at this height would generally have a more pleasing appearance than those with flattish heads of flower.

If, however, small groups of, say, three plants of a kind are used, it would be quite permissible to place some which have a good overall appearance nearer the front than their flowering height would suggest. Kniphofias are a specially good example; they have good foliage and erect spikes. To place a group of a variety which flowers at, say, 3½ ft. (100 cm.) in the centre of a bed 6–8 ft. (180–240 cm.) wide would be a mistake if it could not be seen more or less entire because of a 3 ft. (90 cm.) michaelmas daisy placed in front of it. The same mistake could be made in positions nearer the front and wherever possible one does well to study the habits of plants so that those with a good overall appearance—erectly graceful when in flower and neat or well foliaged at other times—should stand out above lower growing kinds with a greater summer spread. This kind of thoughtful planning, regardless of the size of groups or area of bed, helps greatly towards a more natural, less regimented and therefore more pleasing appearance.

It may well be that in planning one's own bed, not all the subjects chosen beforehand will fit in. One may have selected too many of kinds of a certain height, habit, colour, or time of flowering. But the planner has the final choice —unlike those who follow the stereotyped plans some-times offered in catalogues. These are pretty useless, for they take no account of variations in soils, area or situation, nor are they likely to be made up by the seller of kinds which are fully reliable or satisfying. Some professional 'landscape gardeners' also plan beds or borders for clients, but in my experience very few of them have a wide or practical knowledge of plants and will mostly confine their selection to their own favourites, with repetitions making up for their lack of acquaintance with the variety that exists. There is such a wealth of variety in hardy plants that those who wish to make the best of it and to obtain most value are strongly advised to do their own planning. If they find their first list of chosen subjects proves inadequate, they can be quite sure that any group spaces remaining empty can be satisfactorily filled by alternative kinds of a suitable height, habit, colour or flowering period.

There is one big consolation for those who tackle their own planning in fear or trepidation of making mistakes, and it is that errors that appear after the first flowering season can easily be corrected. It can indeed add to the interest taken in the project to find out, as each kind comes into flower, whether or not one's judgement has been correct. And if it should be that certain kinds are misplaced, if they are too tall or too dwarf, if they do not blend nor otherwise please the eye or one's personal sense of fitness, then make a note of it when the discrepancy appears. Study the general pattern of the bed, and if it is considered that, for better effect, changes should be made by swopping over one group for another, it can be done without loss when autumn comes. In such an event, the earlier in autumn the better, and if the soil is not shaken from the roots the plants will scarcely feel the move at all.

This brings up another important point—the best

time for planting a new bed. Assuming that adequate preparations have been made, the best time undoubtedly is in early autumn. The soil is warm, and new roots form quickly to give plants a quick start. It is not, however, certain that an order given to a nurseryman will be delivered at the ideal time of early October. He may well have a large pile-up of such orders and be obliged to send in rotation according to the date on which he received the order. A dry autumn may well make lifting orders difficult. This may begin in late September, or it may be physically impossible to lift plants from dry soil until well into October. There is, however, no need to despond if a delay should occur, because the most important factor, assuming the plants are of good quality, is to plant them in favourable soil conditions. In light soils there is seldom any problem, even if there has been recent rain and if planting has to be delayed into November. The soil is still warm, especially if it has been dug earlier on, but one should be careful not to tread in too firmly late in the year.

It is common knowledge that whatever one plants in the open, roots, whether fibrous or fleshy, should be spread out in a hole of adequate depth. In all cases, pull loose soil in, around, and above the roots and with a little pressure; all will be well if more loose soil is pulled with fingers or rake, so that a tilth is left around the plants. On handling any kind of hardy plant, the depth at which it was growing can be noticed, and one should aim to insert it slightly deeper—no more than half an inch—than what appears to indicate the natural soil level. If avoidable, on heavy or sticky soils planting is best not done too soon after rain. If there is any danger of panning or of soil being picked up on one's shoes, then the use of two or three short boards on which to tread is strongly advised. Footmarks in heavy sticky soil may hold water and injure plants if a sudden frost should come.

Spring planting calls for a somewhat different approach and it is often safer to wait until spring on heavy soils, when by March the upper layer is beginning to dry off. Light soil dries out much more quickly and I have known years when by April plants needed watering in. In all cases, autumn or spring, a consignment of plants should be unpacked immediately it is received and, if dry, roots should be dipped in water and then stood upright, placing them in a sheltered corner away from sun and drying wind. This is all the more important if for some reason planting has to be delayed, but they will keep safely for several weeks if stood up and bedded in damp sand or peat. Later planting in dry conditions is safe if sensible methods of watering are employed. If on making holes for planting the soil is so dry that it tends to run back, then puddling is the answer. This is done either by filling up a hole with water from a can and inserting the plant after it has soaked down, or by half-filling the hole with loose soil after inserting the plant and then filling up with water. Always leave it until the water has soaked down and then pull round more loose soil, firm and rake level. The second method is to use a fine spray, if water pressure is strong enough, taking care that it has moistened the soil to a reasonable depth and plant as the surface begins to dry again. This method can also be successfully used if a dry spell follows planting, but the worst possible means of watering is to splash it about. This can do more harm than good, for often it fails to reach the roots of plants which badly need it, and instead erodes the soil, leaving a surface crust on top as it dries.

One thing more remains to be said and it concerns quality in relation to the price one pays for plants. When one sees offers in the press at prices far below those in the catalogues of specialist producers of hardy plants, there must be, especially for some would-be gardeners, a temptation to go for the cheapest. Not many of the kinds in my descriptive list are ever offered in the large display press advertisements, but if any are, they are almost certain to be immature seedlings and the like. The difference in quality or size one is likely to receive is far greater than the difference in price, and if they are only a quarter the price of a well-grown plant from a reputable specialist producer who issues a catalogue, they are dear in comparison. The latter is not a profiteer, and it is the cheapjacks who make fat profits from gullible purchasers, which enable them to spend large sums on eye-catching advertisements.

# 4
## *Wider Uses for Perennials*

———◦❋◦———

ALTHOUGH THE EMPHASIS in this book is so much on the value of island beds, in order to make the most of hardy perennials, the island bed principle is capable of much wider application. Even the term 'hardy perennials', can be broadened in this sense to include many rock garden plants, shrubs and heathers, including subjects which require special treatment. Amongst the latter, heathers come to mind, along with lime hating and shade- or moisture-loving subjects. And although one would need a very large garden indeed to consider all these, the basic principle of island beds, even if in miniature through lack of space, time or funds, allows more gardeners wider scope in keeping with their particular leanings or favourites.

The still popular sink or trough garden is a miniature island bed. Such receptacles are scarce and expensive and a much larger area could accommodate a considerably wider range at far less cost, if a raised bed were built as a fixture. The walls need be no more than about 2 ft. (60 cm.) high, using old brick, rock or stones, with or without cement or peat blocks. The cheapest of the more permanent materials would probably be concrete blocks and even these should not be disdained if nothing more pleasing can be afforded. They could be rendered or toned down to a less harsh appearance. What matters most is the plants grown within, and an important factor is that one has all-round access to the beds which are easier to maintain and certainly better for whose who dislike bending to ground-level to see their treasures.

Such raised alpine beds can be at any required height and with a little ingenuity can be built so as to leave wall spaces for plants preferring shade of the north side, or extra warmth on the south. Some will grow just in crevices whilst others will drape a wall by cascading from above so that much less of the construction itself is seen. Generally the soil mix for such a bed needs to be gritty and well drained, but peaty pockets can easily be arranged—all providing the mixture is weed free to begin with.

The top need have no rocks; alpine plants grow quite well without them and they take up space. Generally the shape of such a bed should be formal—a rectangle, oval or otherwise—evenly rounded.

Where peat blocks are used for making walls, it is more difficult to achieve the necessary stability. They should be used like bricks, overlapping or binding the joints as best one can. A single block width is not enough except for a very low wall of say, 12 in. (30 cm.) or so high and if making a wall higher than this, the lower courses should be two blocks wide with alternatives of a block endways on for binding. It is likely to be much more secure if the soil mix is shovelled in to keep more or less level with the wall being built, and to have a slight inward slope, the better to withstand the pressure of the soil within. Crevices should also be filled in with soil as building proceeds. In time plant roots will help hold the blocks together, but as peat shrinks with time some rebuilding may be necessary after a few years. Account must also be taken of shrinkage if the peaty mixture is used in the bed itself. This is best countered by an annual top dressing around the plants of gritty peat in which organic fertilizer including potash and phosphate is mixed; it is applied in spring or early autumn.

The plants selected for raised beds should in a general way, be of slow-growing habit except those required for hanging over the wall. Avoid using those that spread quickly by underground shoots, for however pretty they may be, they can become a nuisance by swamping more compact subjects. Even where surface spread is fairly rapid, there is apt to be unfair competition for space unless segregation is practised. These are normal precautions, in keeping with general principles mentioned earlier, but if they are heeded it is true to say that this form of alpine garden, in a mixed bed, enables one to grow a greater variety in a confined space than is possible by any other method.

The 'walkabout' island bed is also worth considering, though it need not be strictly of island form, because access is by means of some form of paving enabling one to reach every part of the bed. The bed should be more or less at ground-level, and the paving need only be like stepping stones, purely as a means of access. The bed can be of any size or shape consistent with the surroundings and can be by way of an adjunct to some other bed and shrubs or plants, or even adjoining a hedge, provided the same kind of pathway makes a boundary space between the two. These pathways or stepping stones—allowing space for creeping or mat-forming plants between—enable the bed to be divided into sections, if one wishes to grow subjects differing in habit, form or soil requirements. The bed can be terraced where the site is on a slope, if only to avoid the erosion likely to occur where slopes are steep. It can be by way of being a composite bed, growing dwarf shrubs, conifers, perennials, bulbs and heathers.

The idea is capable of very wide interpretation—one which gives scope for those with restricted space who crave for variety. It can incorporate a pool with a moisture bed adjoining. Set in a lawn, it can be a feature so charming and interesting for the variety of plants it contains as to be a source of pride and joy to those willing to break with tradition and give vent to their creative instincts.

The pattern of so many gardens is that of a narrow rectangular plot. The central area is lawn, flanked by borders, or else there is a central path with beds or borders on either side. However much the island bed principle may appeal, the owner of such a garden may be daunted when it comes to contemplating a change. In many cases, a full-scale island bed as described in an earlier chapter may be out of the question, simply for lack of space. This is where the midget island bed may be the answer, provided there is room for one not less than 6 ft (180 cm.) wide and 12 ft. (360 cm.) long. Even in this small compass, a fascinating variety of dwarf perennials can be grown. One of a kind may not be enough to make for the bold splashes of colour that are possible in beds large enough to practice grouping; but if variety spells spice for some gardeners, then in a 6 ft. × 12 ft. (180 × 360 cm.) bed they can grow single plants of at least forty kinds and up to twice that number if the selection is of mainly dwarf, slow-spreading subjects.

To prepare, plan and plant a midget island bed calls for the same simple set of rules as does a full-sized one. The tallest plants—not more than 3 ft. (90 cm.) in a 6 ft. (180 cm.) width—should be in the centre and heights graded down to about 6 in. (15 cm.) around the perimeter. It is, of course, even more vital when making a selection of plants for such beds to know in advance the expected height and growth spread. One would have to omit those liable to grow over-tall or with too vigorous a spread. The 6 ft. (180 cm.) delphinium would not only look out of place in a midget bed, but would overshadow its smaller neighbours, as would any over-lusty kind, because light and air are so essential to natural, sturdy growth. And whilst it would be quite in order to include some kinds normally classed as rock garden plants, to enhance the range of dwarfs along the outside, a midget bed should be restricted to perennials. Dwarf shrubs, heathers and most bulbs would not fit in happily, and there is no need to use them since a wide range of perennials is available.

Heathers can be used in island beds, either exclusively or in company with dwarf shrubs and conifers. The raised bed for these is especially valuable for gardens with alkaline soils. Use a lime-free soil made up of peat, leaf-mould mixed with a little loam, and sand if this too is lime-free or neutral. A depth of 2 ft. (60 cm.) is sufficient in which to grow a wide range of ericaceous plants, along with rhododendrons and azaleas and other calcifuges. The lime-tolerant heathers (mainly winter-flowering *Erica carnea* varieties) will grow better where soil is not limey but, as with other raised beds where peat is used, an annual topping up is necessary. Indeed this is advisable where the natural soil is neutral and where a raised bed is unnecessary on this account. This top dressing, best applied in spring after winter-flowering heathers have been trimmed with shears, promotes more luxuriant yet more compact growth, which in turn leads to a better show at flowering time.

For heathers, the island bed has every advantage over

sided borders for much the same reasons as with other hardy perennials. But spacing is of special importance, for heathers grow outwards rather than upwards and do not die back over winter. Allowance must be made for their outward spread if a heather bed is to remain effective for a number of years. Plants obtained from a nursery will be 6 in. (15 cm.) across or less, depending on age and price, but some varieties may cover up to 2 ft. (60 cm.) after two years in good growing conditions. On average, 2 ft. (60 cm.) spacing between plants is about right, but can be varied in keeping with the known rate of spread, usually given in catalogues. Where space permits, grouping is more effective than where single plants of a kind are used and, as with hardy perennials, a little more space should be allowed round each group than between member plants of a group. Special care is needed to avoid quick-growing heathers spoiling other dwarf shrubs or conifers used for the sake of variety.

Since the flowering time of heathers covers most months of the year, if sufficient variety is used, some interspersal adds to interest. There are several, especially the callunas (ling), which have more foliage attraction than when in flower. These too can play their part in making a colourful display along with dwarf flowering shrubs such as daphne, andromeda, polygala, azaleas, etc., but to grow a full range of subjects which have a dislike of lime, part of a bed should be in broken shade other than that from low overhanging trees.

Peat blocks are, of course, highly suitable for raised beds for subjects preferring lime-free soil. The roots of heathers would soon hold a low wall together, though this would not prevent shrinkage and wastage of the peat itself, and after a few years an extra course of blocks might be needed. Using the island bed principles, one would naturally plant the low-growing kinds near the outer edges and in such a position they will tend to drape the wall, even if this is not built with peat blocks. A slight elevation should be made when an island bed is prepared, even if no wall is needed. This would apply where the natural soil has a low lime content. Such soils are often sandy, or they may be of quite heavy texture, but unless the soil is already peaty, ample peat should be dug in at the outset. And a coating of peat of 1–2 in. (3–5 cm.) soon after planting will do a power of good, as well as keeping down weeds. Sedge or heather peat blocks are readily available for wall building, but generally speaking moss peat is best for digging in and top dressing. The latter is cheaper to buy in dried bales and should, of course, be broken down and moistened, bearing in mind that it will absorb about eight times its own weight of water.

There are various ways of growing moisture-loving plants where the natural soil is too dry for them. If space permits, an island bed, with or without a pool, could be devoted to them. Moisture requirements of such plants vary considerably, from those that grow best in fully saturated soil, to those that languish only if the soil becomes dry. In my opinion, a pool as a garden feature without plants growing in the water and around the margins has a very artificial appearance, whereas it is so easy to make it a centre for luxuriance and colour. The prefabricated pool seldom allows for marginal plants, but if it is let in a few inches below ground-level, and placed with dead-level edges, a little overflow will keep the soil moist for a foot or two at least all around. Stones or bricks placed around the rim will prevent soil from sliding into the water, though they will not impede the overflow of water into the soil. In this way a pool, whether prefabricated or contrived by using heavy-gauge poly-thene sheeting, can become the centre-piece of an island bed.

With polythene sheeting, depth of water can be chosen simply by excavating, and the surrounding moisture bed—not necessarily all the way round—is determined by the lip of polythene which spreads the overflow into the soil. This lip, or overlay, need be only a few inches wide, but it should be covered by up to 1 ft. (30 cm.) depth of soil, again held back by bricks, rocks or peat blocks placed on the polythene just where it levels off. Where no pool is required and an area is to be devoted entirely to moisture-loving plants, the sheet of polythene should be laid almost flat as well as level, with a turn-up of 3–4 in. (8–10 cm.) around the edge, just to prevent rain or applied water from escaping too quickly into the subsoil. This pan should not be less than 1 ft. (30 cm.) underground and 2 ft. (60 cm.) would not be too deep. Bearing in mind the varying moisture require-ments of plants, part of the area should be punctured with small holes to allow partial drainage for subjects dis-liking permanent saturation below the roots.

This is a subject with many variables, affected by both climate and the type of soil and subsoil of a given site. It would be unwise to embark on a scheme without know-ing in advance every possible factor which might affect success or failure. In the past I have recommended sub-irrigation by means of a grid made up of land drain pipes. These are quite cheap to buy and are made of baked clay. They can be laid end to end on the level about 12–14 in. (30–6 cm.) below the surface, so con-nected as a grid that they can be filled in dry periods from a hole placed in an upended feeder pipe. This method is reliable, but the space between the rows of pipes would need to vary from 3–5 ft. (90–150 cm., depending on how quickly the subsoil absorbs the water leaking from the joints of the pipes. Four-inch (10 cm.) diameter pipes are about right.

For a very small area, and where a small collection of moisture-loving plants is grown as part of a larger bed, land drain pipes can be especially useful. One pipe of 4 in. (10 cm.) diameter can be the means of applying extra moisture to the roots of three plants of robust growth, and more than three if it is placed in the centre of several dwarf kinds. The pipe should be let upright into the ground, so that no more than an inch of its upper rim is visible. Foliage will hide it from view during the growing season and if the pipe is filled up with water much of it will reach the roots of the plants—and it is always the roots which need the moisture. Overhead watering has its snags, especially on the heavier soils or those which cake when wet. In such soils the upturned pipe will not adversely affect drainage or soil texture, but where drainage into the subsoil is rapid, as is the case in most gravelly and sandy soils, then the base of the pipe should sit in a shallow tin or pan of wider diameter than the pipe. This will then act as a little reservoir and will make for far less frequent filling of the drain pipe.

There are so many beautiful subjects appreciative of extra moisture that one misses out if no attempt is made to grow them. Because of the variables, some experimentation is often worth while and the upturned land drain is therefore recommended. It can be employed as an experiment before embarking on a larger scheme or, where only a small area can be devoted to such plants, it can be a permanent, reliable and simple means to an end.

In my own garden, with ample space and with largely informal outlines, undulations and established trees, many island beds include all the plants mentioned in this chapter, and there are also beds where perennials are used exclusively. Altogether, the 5–6 acres (2·02–2·43 ha.) covered holds about fifty island beds, some being quite large. I am not ashamed to admit that, in the process of breaking with convention and in giving vent to imagination, as well as in experimenting, I have made some mistakes. In the process I have been able to learn and profit by these mistakes. The knowledge thus gained is passed on to readers with the suggestion that if they too, make mistakes these will not be serious enough to deflect them from this mode of gardening, which I have found so rewarding.

# 5
## *Making the Best of Restrictions*

A LARGE NUMBER of garden-owners still possess a conventional one-sided backed border. A few may be quite content with it, but others, who have not replaced it with shrubs, may feel themselves stuck with a problem they shrink from trying to solve. These old-type borders have a built-in capacity for self-strangulation. It takes place insidiously, especially if any of the extra maintenance they demand is neglected. Apart from the basic fault of depriving plants of ample light and air, more often than not the borders were made far too narrow for the heights reached by some of their contents. Some of these tall-growing plants, such as solidago (golden rod), helianthus (perennial sunflower) and other members of the daisy tribe, become hungry for space as well as nutriment and as they encroach they deprive choicer kinds, which may be less tall, of both vital sustenance and space at ground-level and above. Unless annual curbs are made, the taller plants steadily take over; such curbing, to be effective, involves frequent replanting, if only to prevent deterioration in the display of these aggressive kinds. These remarks, resulting from seeing so many unsightly and unworthy conventional borders, are made to emphasize not only the advantages of island beds, but also the importance of careful selection for any kind of bed or border. Any plants with aggressive or invasive tendencies, even if these are otherwise attractive in flower, should be used only with care and caution.

The only remedy for an overgrown or neglected herbaceous border is to begin again. If there are no perennial weeds such as couch or ground elder which must first be destroyed, most fibrous-rooted, but worn-out or invasive perennials can be safely dug in if trenched. As most people realise, this need not entail double digging with the second spit brought on top and the first spit, including rubbish, underneath. It can be accomplished by opening a trench at one end and taking a few barrow-loads to fill in at the other when finished. Old plants, to be discarded, should be dug out to carry as little soil as possible and added to any manure or compost to be turned over in the bottom of a 9–10 in. (23–5 cm.) trench, topside down. The alternative, and this may also apply when not using chemicals on perennial weeds, is to dig the bed over to a depth of 5–6 in. (13–15 cm.), using a fork to shake both plants and weeds free of soil. If this can be done in summer, twice where very weedy, sun and wind will do the killing, leaving the ground ready for straightforward digging and composting in autumn. Naturally, any plants worth keeping to use in a replant-ing scheme would be lifted as a first step and heeled in for later use. If such plants are themselves free of obnoxious perennial weeds, there is good reason for tak-ing care of them, but even the tiniest piece of ground elder or couch lurking amongst a plant's roots will also be given a new lease of life and cause renewed trouble within a year or two.

Having decided to have done with an old herbaceous border, the mind can then be more receptive to new ideas, thus avoiding repetition of former mistakes. Should the one-sided border formation still appeal, if

Alpines and conifers on a sloping island bed.

Alpines and conifers bed on the left slope, perennials on the right. Early summer.

Looking down on an island bed (in shade at the far end) showing grouping for height with the tallest subjects in the centre

Overall view of beds with the tallest plants in the centre. June.
Restricted use of rock allows a more effective use of plants.

Looking over one island bed to another beyond, showing the advantage of background effects.

Island beds with background of evergreens.

A stone-built garden shelter and a weeping willow make a background to this island bed.

The rounded end of an island bed showing a spiky but graceful *Cimicifuga*

The small bed in the centre is flanked by a long bed of alpines, conifers and heathers.

Island beds with conifers as a background to break the uniformity.

Overall view of two island beds taken in early summer.

Overall view of an island bed in late May.

Close-up of terraced shade-plant section with the rare double white
*Trillium grandiflorum plenum* near the centre of the picture. Late spring.

An island bed taken from above and showing dwarf subjects nearest the path.

A view overlooking island beds, taken from the top of the terraced bank.

only because the garden offers too little scope for an island bed, the main concern should be the effective width of the old bed and a resolve to make a selection in keeping with it, and to choose the most worthy subjects with which to plant it. The rule of having the maximum height of subjects limited to about half the width of the border (the taller plants being placed mainly at the back) should still apply. But it is the effective width that matters and this is determined by the backing. Whether this consists of a wall, fence, or hedge, its influence on plant growth must be taken into account, and in any case it is a mistake to place closely to it plants which form part of the general collection. A wall or fence would be best used for quite a different selection to include those of a more shrubby nature that grow best against a wall or fence, and others, including bulbs, which will leave some space for light and air after they have flowered. In other words, there should be a space left at the rear to provide both access and air.

Where the backing is of a hedge, then a space is all the more vital because, apart from other considerations, depending on the hedge's size or age, its roots are bound to have an adverse effect on those plants within their reach. The same applies where evergreens, (other than as a hedge) form a background, or where, as is sometimes the case, a border backs up to fruit or other deciduous trees. Any such trees or shrubs, if well established, will have far-ranging roots and these will quickly make a beeline for newly dug and enriched soil within their reach. I have a bed designed to take advantage of a large tree 12 yds. (11 m) from its nearest edge and have often found roots which in one season have penetrated 3–4 yds. (2·70–3·60 m). into the bed.

Hedge roots are usually much less wide-ranging than

those of mature trees and though no less hungry, are easier to keep in check, so long as the vital space between hedge and border is made at the outset. How wide this space should be must be a matter of discretion, when one has found by digging the extent of the roots, outward penetration a foot or so down, at, say, 2 ft. (60 cm.) away. This is about the minimum space that should be allowed away from the base of a hedge, and if it were made an annual task during winter to dig the width of a spade along the edge of the strip next to the plants in the border, all should be well. The spade must, of course, be used at sufficient depth to sever the roots of the hedge at this point, and it can be done in the knowledge that whereas the hedge will not suffer if it *is* done, the plants in the border undoubtedly will if it is not.

The next thing to consider, when dealing with an old herbaceous border, is the possibility of it being widened.

Constricted width means a restricted selection of plants, and it may be that a permanently solid path prevents any widening but in many instances a greater width can be made, especially if a border fronts directly on to a lawn. Where it is bounded by a gravel or paving, it would be worth the effort. Gravel is not usually laid thickly on a garden path and when damp a fork will penetrate; with deep digging the mixed-in sand and stones will do no harm and it might well do good, where the underlying soil is heavy, by improving drainage.

If a few feet can be added to the width of a one-sided border, it can become an island bed, no matter what its aspect is. If such an addition allows rear access, against the backing, then the harmful effect of the latter on plant growth will be greatly reduced, if not cancelled out altogether. If the backing is of a wall or fence, it may well serve a new and useful purpose. There is a wealth of variety of shrubby subjects which prefer to be against a wall, especially if this faces a southerly direction, and if space permits, a narrow border—1–2 ft. (30–60 cm.) wide—would make a perfect home for lowlier plants or bulbs with a similar preference, many of which would not survive if planted in an exposed position. A fence would offer less scope in this respect, and though there are some dwarf plants or bulbs adaptable for growing on a strip fronting a hedge, ground-covering subjects would generally be most suitable.

A backing with a northerly aspect would naturally call for a very different selection. A few wall shrubs for shade can be used, but any shady strip at the foot can be occupied by quite a number of dwarf plants, including carpeters. These mostly flower in spring and the reason why dwarfness is emphasized for strips against a backing is that anything tall would tend to be lanky and outward lolling. It is worth reflecting that if an island bed is created by widening an existing one-sided border, it is not essential to have the tallest kinds in the centre, as is advised with an island bed well in the open.

I have two fairly large island beds on the north side of a shelter belt of Portugal laurels which are up to 16 ft. (480 cm.) or so high. I planned these so that a 3 ft. (90 cm.) wide path was left next to them, but shade from them extended beyond this. The subjects planted next to the path were mainly dwarf and spring flowering such as pulmonarias, epimediums, primulas and bergenias, as frontal groups, and behind them a variety of taller kinds which preferred some shade. These flower later, but whereas from the rear path there is plenty of interest in flower from March to May, after that it is the view from the far side of the bed which provides the colour.

This idea can be practised with a south-facing aspect,

because whilst one still has an island bed, the tallest kinds placed beyond the halfway or central positions will provide some shade to the dwarf spring-flowering plants beyond. It is from May onwards that shade-loving subjects need protection from strong sunlight and by late May most tall-growing plants have sufficient height to give some shade to dwarf kinds growing in a strip beside the path which divides the backing from the bed.

This rear path need not be wider than is necessary (a) for access, (b) to allow a free circulation of air in the growing season, and (c) to be out of harmful reach of roots coming from a hedge or other live backing. In the conventional herbaceous border, so often crammed and inaccessible, it is the lack of rear space that causes so much trouble and disappointment. Those willing and able to make the break with convention by creating a break at the back of a one-sided border will be well rewarded.

As a break from concentration on the back of the border, a little should be said about the front. Any plan where a front line has to be drawn between a bed and a border should take account of environmental factors. A temptation to go in for zigzags and scalloped edges should be resisted, but if gentle curves appeal, these can scarcely offend anyone's sense of fitness. If the general pattern of a garden and its surroundings consists of straight lines, then a curving front can harmonize, and for an island bed in an oblong rectangle of a lawn, an oval shape or straight sides and semicircular ends will fit in well, as would a circle in a roughly square lawn.

Beds of quite informal shape match in best with environmental informality, such as exists at Bressingham. Here I found that the shape of a border was easily, and to my mind naturally, determined by the lie of the land and position of the trees which someone planted a couple of centuries earlier. Many of these beds are somewhat kidney shaped, with continuous but gentle curves, and straight-fronted beds were made only to match up with a rear wall, which was likewise straight. One retaining wall I built of local flint faces south-west and has a bed for sun and moisture-lovers at the foot, and one of plants that prefer it dry on top. Another version of this idea, as a means of using slopes too steep without a terracing wall, is to plant up with erect growing plants on top to the south; these keep strong sunlight from the shade and moisture-loving kinds below.

These examples underline the ways in which existing conditions of slope, aspect and environment can make it possible to draw upon the immense variety of plants in existence. One may not at first see the full potential existing within the confines of a given space; but given an open mind, as well as an awareness of the diversity and the adaptability of plants, a way may suddenly appear either of making the best use of some baffling or problematical part of the garden, or of growing kinds of plants which need the out-of-the-ordinary treatment one has previously had to dismiss as out of reach. Sometimes both needs can be fulfilled.

Such variations may fall outside the more usual range of plants which prefer an open position in ordinary soil, as do the majority. The minority fall into such categories as lime-haters and moisture- and shade-lovers, though all too often there is a need in gardens for plants which will flourish in dry shade under trees. I have known a certain amount of irritation and lack of understanding to be shown when I have been trying to explain that dry shade offers the least scope of all for hardy plants, but this is one area which the evolution of plants has failed to adapt to. It is understandable because all living things need food and drink in some form or other, and where trees are established, with a root system as widespread below the ground as twigs and branches above, few plants in nature could have adapted themselves to such under-nourishment. There are such kinds, but the variety is limited, as is the display they give.

# 6

## Obtaining Long Term Rewards from Perennials

No MATTER BY what means one grows hardy plants, year-by-year maintenance should follow a similar pattern. I was taken to task for using the title *Perennials for Trouble-Free Gardening* for one of my books. Perhaps it should have been 'for Less Troublesome' instead of 'Trouble-Free'. In one sense there is, I freely admit, no such thing as trouble-freedom in gardening of any kind. My aim in both that book (1960) and this is to show ways and means of reducing trouble in its true sense— that of onerous and unrewarding work or effort. I maintain that with a sensible approach, a good beginning with a suitable site for the plants one wishes to grow, hardy plants are very rewarding indeed. The work involved in preparation, planning and planting on sound lines will show a saving in work and trouble year after year, if certain basic essentials regarding maintenance are practised.

These essentials are not so much a case of laying down a complicated set of rules, of 'do' and 'don't' and 'if', but are towards an understanding of the nature of plants under varying conditions of soil, climate or season, so as to minimize trouble. Interest with understanding and knowledge are self-complementary, each adding to the other, in practically every human endeavour, and this is certainly true in the realm of plants in which the well of knowledge to be gained is inexhaustible. The better the understanding and the wider the knowledge, the greater the interest is given in return. The truth of this is apparent, even if after we have learned quite a lot we come to the point when we realize how little we know compared with what more there is to learn. It is at the point when we can accept that 100 per cent success with all we grow year after year is likely to remain elusive, that we may also realize how absorbing and satisfying an interest plants are.

Very little needs to be done in the first season after planting a new bed or border, apart from frequent hoeing during the growing season. It stands to reason that when seedling weeds appear, the smaller they are when the hoe is applied, the quicker they will die, leaving no trace. It also makes sense to watch out for any pernicious perennial weeds which reappear, lurking amongst the roots of plants, possibly due to imperfect site preparation. It is again best to be rid of even the tiniest piece of couch or ground elder without delay, rather than let it grow and spread.

I have already mentioned the advisability of making notes during the growing season if some error or misplacement of a certain kind shows up, so that when the planting season comes round again, the necessary adjustments can be made. If planting has been made to a plan, this too should be altered and for those who do not wish to label each kind, the plan can be referred to whenever a check in identification is needed. Labelling is, of course, a matter of personal choice, but many a gardener whose interest has subsequently developed has wished that some permanent means of identification had been used from the beginning. At the time, botanic names may have seemed unnecessary and burdensome, but very few who become really interested in plants find them difficult once their value and usefulness is accepted. Those who try to persist in using common names, such as bellflower for campanula and yarrow for achillea will run into far greater difficulties than by using the generic and specific. No one boggles at chrysanthemum and rhododendron and it is when one grows such good hardy plants as cimicifuga and rudbeckia that these and many more become easy through recognition and usage.

A note here on nomenclature may allay suspicions that some names I have used are out of date. In some cases I have quite deliberately employed specific names, knowing that they have been supplanted. This is in defence of common usage, for I see no point in keeping strictly to the rules by which taxonomists work, thus involving changes, when such changes are liable to confuse the gardening public. A name which has become well known and accepted should be allowed to stand in horticultural circles, since the viewpoint of botanists and that of gardeners is mostly poles apart.

A droughty period may occur in the first year after planting a new bed or border. An autumn planting is much less likely to suffer than planting left till spring, and as some compensation, heavy soils retain moisture longer than light. The one danger with heavy soil occurs when clots, however small, have not been broken down into tilth at the time of planting. Old-year digging on heavy soil will allow winter frosts and spring winds to break down clots; if they are not broken, then sun and wind in later spring can penetrate into the soil and affect new plantings.

If it is dry at planting time the puddling method can be repeated in a modified way later on if plants are suffering. The top inch or two around plants can be drawn back and the depression filled with water, replacing the top tilth after it has soaked in. The tilth is important, because an artificially watered surface will cake and hinder capillary action, whereas tilth fosters it. Subsequent puddlings would be troublesome on any large-scale plantings, and provided there is sufficient pressure, a fine misty spray sprinkler will be far simpler. Tests should be made to avoid overwatering as well as to ensure that enough moisture has been applied to penetrate to the feeding roots of plants. Overwatering is always harmful, making for soil compression and loss of structure. Soil which cannot breathe, as it were, will not promote plant growth, and this, too, underlines the harm caused by haphazard splashings of water over the surface with a can or from the end of a hose.

In subsequent years there is little to be feared from dry weather except that a severe drought, especially on light soils, could shorten the flowering season and cause withering of the lower leaves of some plants. The older such plants become, the more liable they are to fall short of their best, but if water is available with sufficient pressure it should always be applied in the finest possible spray, as late as possible in the day. Other methods of irrigation should be mentioned, because quite often pressure from the mains supply is too low for a spray sprinkler to be effective. Trickle irrigation pipes, usually of plastic, can be bought quite cheaply. These have small holes at intervals so that with a connection to a tap, water escapes through the holes and on to the soil so gently that most of the tilth is retained. This method is one which helps to cut down waste such as occurs with overhead sprinklers when sun and wind can have a dissipating effect. Trickle irrigation is, however, not without its snags. The pipe will moisten only about a foot wide on either side and, even though it is light in weight, care and patience are needed to move it between growing plants so that the next strip can be watered.

These remarks apply to any collection of hardy plants which have no special moisture requirements—those belonging to the majority which prefer an open situation and grow in ordinary soil. These can be relied upon to give a good display in any but abnormally long dry spells of weather. There are, however, certain kinds which one might wish to include and which suffer from lack of moisture to a greater extent, in keeping with their natural habitat. Whenever such plants—trollius, ranunculus, astilbes, and so on—are included as a small part of a collection, there is a very simple method of apply water to the roots. Land drain pipes are easily obtainable and if one of these, or even a cocoa tin with holes in the bottom and lower sides, is inserted, it can serve to keep about three moisture-loving plants happy during a drought. It should be filled with water every day or two, and if the top tin is at about ground-level it will not obtrude.

Almost all moisture-loving plants like a humus-rich soil. Peat is the easiest form of humus to obtain and apply, and as a mulch or top dressing it will do a power of good by keeping the moisture in. It keeps the soil cool as well as enriching it, especially if preceded by a dusting of organic fertilizer. Well-made compost can take the place of peat as a mulch, but it is less helpful in weed control.

It is true to say that any soil which is not already peaty or with a high humus content will be improved by the addition of peat as a surface mulch, and all but the comparatively few kinds of plants which prefer hot, dry conditions will benefit from it. It has often been said that mulching should not be practised until spring growth is well under way, because it retards the returning warmth to the soil. The discovery has fairly recently been made, however, that soil temperatures are much higher in the last three months of the year than in the April–June period. This tends to counter the old dictum, and as far as my experience goes, autumn and early winter are the best times for mulching. With plenty of compost available, I use it liberally on such subjects as astilbes, hostas, heucheras, phlox and anything that appreciates good living, or tends to grow woody rooted in time. The main objective is to provide extra nutriment for near surface roots and so build up the general fertility along with the soil level. Like peat, compost is an expendable material and though it is also used for digging in before planting, its benefits as a mulch are obvious when summer comes again, from the point of view of fertility and also of moisture retention.

Peat is equally effective, but by itself has less fertility, though it is perhaps a better soil conditioner. For this reason, I dust some organic or compound fertilizer around plants before applying a peat mulch, making sure, of course, that any weeds which may grow through are first removed. This is a much easier and quicker method than mixing in fertilizer with the peat before it is applied, and there is little risk of any of its vital constituents being leached out by winter rains if the mulching follows the fertilizer immediately. If, however, a high nitrogen fertilizer is called for as a boost, then this would be best applied in spring, just before the first round with the hoe.

It would seem then that a peat mulch can be applied at any time between October and May. Half an inch to an inch is sufficient, and if for any reason summer arrives and it is thought that a peat dressing would help in keeping down weeds and conserving moisture, it can do nothing but good. At any time it is easier to apply if moistened sufficiently to avoid dustiness, but a more thorough wetting would be needed for late spring or early summer. Peat already moistened is available in bags, but since it absorbs up to eight times its dry weight when moist the decision has to be made on the economics of buying bone-dry baled peat or ready-to-apply moist from bags, and there is not much to choose in value between the sedge and the moss peat varieties. It is the latter that is mostly sold dry in bales, which has to be broken down, watered and turned a few times before sufficient water is absorbed. It must be a matter of discretion, according to the nature of the soil, whether and to what extent mulching is an annual, biennial or triennial task, but there would be very little trace left of a mulch after the second year.

Staking and rejuvenating where necessary are the only other maintenance operations that need be considered. Staking can be dismissed altogether where island beds are concerned if the section they contain will stand unaided, as most will. There are of course, some kinds such as delphiniums, which may well be regarded as indispensable, which are all too easily laid low by strong winds and storms. As they reach the flowering stage, the weight of the flower spike increases and top-heaviness develops, so something has to give and it is usually the lower part of the stem. Such weakness is largely due to breeding developments, in which the size of flower, the number of petals and the length of spike have been the criteria for improvement on the original species. Natural selection in evolutionary matters tend to work the other way—that of ensuring the safest means of perpetuating the species.

Staking can be dealt with by passing on the cures. If a selection of perennials with naturally strong stems is made, there need be no staking in island beds or well-planned borders. There need be none if the owner chooses certain kinds which, though weak in the stem, reach no great height and naturally do not grow erectly. These, to my mind, have a better appearance if left to loll as they wish, so long as they do not overhang or spoil their neighbours. *Alchemilla mollis*, some hardy geraniums and some potentillas are examples, none of which exceed about 2 ft. (60 cm.) in height; their effect would be spoiled by supports. As for taller subjects, including delphiniums, the most important factor—apart from the effectiveness of the type of support, be it canes, peasticks or metal rings on stalks—is that of timing. If ever the adage about 'shutting the stable door' applies other than to absentee horses, it certainly does to the necessity of staking plants in good time. If not done until the plants topple, no amount of trouble will restore them to positions they would have been in had supports been used whilst they were still erect and growing. In some parts and in some soils, certain kinds would need supporting when in drier, poorer soils they would not. I have supplied a list of perennials which generally need no staking, but it must remain a matter of discretion when it comes to practice. A new bed would provide indications of what to expect when it is fully established in the second season.

The one remaining maintenance task is not likely to occur until a new planting scheme is three years old. It concerns attention to certain kinds which would benefit from replanting, either through soil exhaustion, or because they produce too many flowering stems for the plant to bring to perfection. In a few cases there is a tendency for plants which form crowns to grow somewhat out of the ground, such as astilbes, geums and heucheras benefit from mulching for this reason, for it encourages feeding roots to form, thereby helping the plants to retain vigour. It is, however, unreasonable to infer that this is the best or only remedy in the long term. Such kinds are very easy to divide and if loss of vigour or flowering quality becomes apparent, an alternative to mulching—which might not have been practised anyway—is to replant the healthiest pieces more deeply, after the space has been dug and fertilized. Excess woody root should be discarded.

Soil exhaustion is a different matter and it is sometimes a case of plants becoming over-congested. It occurs mostly in certain quick-growing members of the daisy family (*Compositae*) especially with *Aster Nova Belgii* (michaelmas daisy), heleniums and helianthus and a few more. Again, the remedy is to replant with smaller pieces in enriched soil; though this is also the group of plants which often produce too many flowering stems, the alternative of thinning some out is rather tiresome. It would have to be done in early summer, or at least a month before flowering time. A third group contains kinds such as geraniums and monardas which make a fairly rapid annual spread and these would need curbing every two or three years to prevent them from spoiling neighbouring groups; there are not many of these and replanting is generally the best way of confining them. A few can be reduced by forking out any excessive spread, whether one is dealing with the surface growth of such plants as monarda, or with those which creep just below surface, as do macleaya and physostegia. Unwanted pieces are best taken out with a narrow-tined fork, after severing with a spade any which have wandered outside the group's perimeter.

This kind of maintenance is not likely to be onerous, if it is not neglected when the signs come that attention is needed. It may well involve less than 10 per cent replanting per annum and, for the good results it brings, this is not a high price in terms of maintenance costs. Young healthy plants of this type will generally have a longer period in flower than when old and congested. If it is looked upon as a natural outcome—because one is growing a collection of plants with a diversity of habits, which are in all other respects content to be placed in a confined space far removed from their native habitat—it becomes not a chore but an interesting labour of love, of caring for plants as if they were pets, sometimes a little wayward, and in need of control or encouragement.

When discussing such matters as the need for staking and for rejuvenating, it must be remembered that plants are liable to some variation in different soils and districts. For example, a rich soil in a high rainfall area is bound to induce more growth or stem length than does a drier soil.

I have tried to make it clear that care and maintenance, season by season, should not therefore be a matter of hard-and-fast rules, but of following through the basic principles by which one began, constantly learning something in the process, even if by trial and error. My advice on this subject would be valueless if I had not made some mistakes during my fifty years with hardy plants, but there would be very little point in writing a book which failed to pass on certain conclusions I have reached, with regard to care and maintenance, together with my assessments of the garden-worthiness of plants described. The most rational approach is that which fosters interest as well as reduces work, but to those who become most keenly interested in plants, essential maintenance becomes pleasurable rather than troublesome, giving satisfaction for the mind and health for the body.

*Selected Lists*
*of Plants for Special Purposes*

The plants listed should be obtained from reliable Nurseries specializing in perennials. All are obtainable, by mail order only, from Bressingham Gardens, Diss, Norfolk.

# I *A Selection of Alpines, Dwarf Shrubs and Small Herbaceous Perennials for Peaty Soil*

*Those marked S. best in some shade.*
*N.L.F. denotes neutral or lime-free soil.*
*Heights not given for prostrate or mat-forming kinds.*

*Acorus gramineus*, 6–8 in. (15–20 cm.)
*Adiantum venustum*, S. (fern) and most other dwarf ferns,
 6 in. (15 cm.)
Adonis
*Ajuga pyramidalis*, S., 10 in. (25 cm.)
Andromeda in variety, N.L.F., 10–20 in. (25–50 cm.)
Asplenium (ferns) in variety, S., 10–24 in. (25–60 cm.)
Astilbe, dwarf kinds, S., 6–12 in. (15–30 cm.)
*Caltha leptosepala*, 6 in. (15 cm.)
Chiastophyllum (Cotyledon), 6 in. (15 cm.)
*Chrysogonum virginianum*, N.L.F., 6 in. (15 cm.)
Codonopsis in variety
Cortusa, S., 6 in. (15 cm.)
*Cyananthus lobatus*, S., N.L.F.
Cyclamen, S., 4–8 in. (10–20 cm.)
*Deinanthe coerulea*, S., N.L.F.
Disporum, S., N.L.F.
Dodecatheon, S., 8–12 in. (20–30 cm.)
*Epimedium* × *youngianum* 'Niveum', S.
*Erythronium californicum* and other species
*Gentiana asclepiadea* and late summer and autumn
 flowering kinds, S., N.L.F.
  4–20 in. (10–50 cm.)

Haberlea, S., 6 in. (15 cm.)
*Hacquetia epipactis*, 6 in. (15 cm.)
Hepatica in variety, S. 4–6 in. (10–15 cm.)
Hosta, dwarf kinds, S.
Helleborus, S.
*Incarvillea grandiflora* 10 in. (25 cm.)
*Lithospermum diffusum*, N.L.F.
*Meconopsis quintuplinervia*, S., 12 in. (30 cm.)
*Mentha requienii*
Omphalodes, S., 4–6 in. (10–15 cm.)
Ophiopogon, 4–8 in. (10–20 cm.)
Orchis in variety
Ourisia, S., N.L.F. 6–8 in. (15–20 cm.)
*Phlox adsurgens*, N.L.F.
    *P. pilosa*, S.
Platycodon
*Polygala chamaebuxus*, N.L.F., 6 in. (15 cm.)
    *P. vayredae*, N.L.F. 6 in. (15 cm.)
*Polygonatum hookeri*, S. 4 in. (10 cm.)
*Polygonum macrophyllum* 16 in. (40 cm.)
    *P. milletii*, 10 in. (25 cm.)
Primula in selected dwarf kinds other than Bog Primulas,
    S., up to 8 in. (20 cm.)
Ramonda, S., 6 in. (15 cm.)
Rhododendron, including azaleas, dwarf kinds, N.L.F.
Saxifraga, selected kinds
Soldanella, S., N.L.F., 4–6 in. (10–15 cm.)
Synthyris, S.
Thalictrum, dwarf kinds, S., 2–8 in. (5–20 cm.)
Tiarella, S., N.L.F., 6–8 in. (15–20 cm.)
Trillium, S.

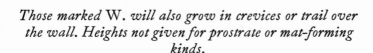

*Those marked* W. *will also grow in crevices or trail over
the wall. Heights not given for prostrate or mat-forming
kinds.*

Achillea, dwarf kinds, 4–8 in. (10–20 cm.)
*Aethionema* 'Warley Rose', 6 in. (15 cm.)
Allium, most dwarf non-invasive kinds, 4–8 in. (10–20
    cm.)
Alyssum in variety, W., 6–9 in. (15–23 cm.)
Androsace in variety
Aquilegia, dwarf kinds, 4–12 in. (10–30 cm.)
Arabis, 4–6 in. (10–15 cm.)
Armeria in variety, W., 4–8 in. (10–20 cm.)
Asperula, compact kinds
Aubrieta in variety
*Campanula carpatica* (syn. *C. turbinata*), 4–8 in. (10–20
    cm.)
    *C. garganica*, W., 4–6 in. (10–15 cm.)
    *C. portenschlagiana* (syn. *C. muralis*), W., 4–6 in.
        (10–15 cm.)
    *C.* × *stansfieldii*, 4–8 in. (10–20 cm.)
    *C.* 'Stella', W., 4–6 in. (10–15 cm.)
*Carduncellus rhaponticoides*, 5 in. (13 cm.)
Cheiranthus, dwarf perennial kinds, 6–12 in. (15–30
    cm.)
*Chiastophyllum oppositifolium* (syn. *Cotyledon simplicifolia*)
    4–6 in. (10–15 cm.)
*Crepis incana*, 12 in. (30 cm.)

Dianthus in variety, W., 3–9 in. (8–23 cm.)
Draba in variety, 2–4 in. (5–10 cm.)
Erinus, 4 in. (10 cm.)
Erodium in variety, 2–8 in. (5–20 cm.)
Gentiana, spring and summer flowering kinds, 3–9 in. (8–23 cm.)
Geranium, most dwarf kinds, 4–6 in. (10–15 cm.)
Globularia in variety, 2–6 in. (5–15 cm.)
Gypsophila, most dwarf kinds
Helianthemum in variety, W., 4–8 in. (10–20 cm.)
Helichrysum, most dwarf kinds
Hypericum, dwarf kinds, W., 2–8 in. (5–20 cm.)
Iberis in variety, W., 4–8 in. (10–20 cm.)
Lewisia in variety (no lime), 4–8 in. (10–20 cm.)
Limonium, dwarf kinds, 4–10 in. (10–25 cm.)
Linum, dwarf kinds, 6–10 in. (15–25 cm.)
Micromeria in variety, 4–8 in. (10–20 cm.)
Moltkia, 6–10 in. (15–25 cm.)
Morisia 2 in. (5 cm.)
*Myosotis rupicola*, 4 in. (10 cm.)
Origanum, compact species, 6–12 in. (15–30 cm.)
Parahebe in variety, 4–10 in. (10–25 cm.)
Penstemon, dwarf kinds, 4–10 in. (10–25 cm.)
*Phlox douglasii* in variety
    *P. subulata* in variety
*Polygonum vaccinifolium*, W.
Potentilla, dwarf kinds, 2–6 in. (5–15 cm.)
Ramonda, W. north facing, 4 in. (10 cm.)
Raoulia
Saponaria, dwarf kinds
*Saxifraga aizoon* in variety, 4–12 in. (10–30 cm.)
Sedum, compact growing kinds, up to 9 in. (up to 23 cm.)
Sempervivum in variety

Silene, 2–6 in. (5–15 cm.)
Thymus, compact kinds
Tunica, 4–8 in. (10–20 cm.)
Veronica, dwarf kinds, up to 9 in. (up to 23 cm.)
Zauschneria, 8–12 in. (20–30 cm.)

*Achillea* 'Moonshine', 20 in. (50 cm.)

*Adonis amurensis* 'Pleniflora', 6 in. (15 cm.)

   *A.* 'Fukujukai', 6 in. (15 cm.)

*Anemone* 'Bressingham Glow', 'September Charm', 20 in. (50 cm.)

*Anthemis rudolphiana*, 20 in. (50 cm.)

   *A. sancti-johannis*, 20 in. (50 cm.)

*Armeria* 'Bees Ruby', 16 in. (40 cm.), 'Dusseldorf', 6 in. (15 cm.)

*Aster* × *frikartii*, 32 in. (80 cm.), 'Jubilee', 20 in. (50 cm.), 'Violet Queen', 20 in. (50 cm.) and others

   *A. novi-belgii* 'Carnival', 24 in. (60 cm.), 'Royal Ruby', 24 in. (60 cm.)

   'Royal Violet', 24 in. (60 cm.)

   *A. thomsonii* 'Nanus', 16 in. (40 cm.)

Aster dwarf hybrids, 'Jenny', 16 in. (40 cm.), 'Lady in Blue', 12 in. (30 cm.), 'Little Pink Beauty', 12 in. (30 cm.) and others

*Campanula alliariifolia* 'Ivory Bells', 18 in. (45 cm.)

   *C.* 'Birch Hybrid', 6 in. (15 cm.)

   *C. carpatica* 'Blue Moonlight', 8 in. (20 cm.), 'Bressingham White', 8 in. (20 cm.), 'Isobel', 10 in. (25 cm.) and others

   *C. glomerata* 'Nana Alba', 16 in. (40 cm.)

   *C.* 'Molly Pinsent', 6 in. (15 cm.)

   *C. portenschlagiana*, 6 in. (15 cm.)

*Centaurea hypoleuca*, 16 in. (40 cm.)

Chiastophyllum (Cotyledon), 6 in. (15 cm.)
*Chrysogonum virginianum*, 6 in. (15 cm.)
*Clematis integrifolia* 'Hendersonii', 20 in. (50 cm.)
*Coreopsis verticillata*, 20 in. (50 cm.)
*Crepis incana*, 16 in. (40 cm.)
*Crocosmia masonorum*, 36 in. (90 cm.)
*Dianthus* 'Mrs Pilkington', or any named 'Pink', 6–10 in.
    (15–25 cm.)
*Dicentra* 'Adrian Bloom', 16 in. (40 cm.)
  *D. spectabilis*, 24 in. (60 cm.)
*Doronicum* 'Spring Beauty', 16 in. (40 cm.)
Erigeron, dwarf varieties, 10–12 in. (25–50 cm.)
*Eryngium bourgatii*, 24 in. (60 cm.)
*Euphorbia polychroma* (syn. *E. epithymoides*), 16 in.
    (40 cm.)
*Filipendula hexapetala* 'Plena', 18–24 in. (45–60 cm.)
*Gentiana septemfida*, 6 in. (15 cm.)
*Geranium* 'Johnson's Blue', 12 in. (30 cm.)
  *G. renardii*, 12 in. (30 cm.)
  *G. subcaulescens*, 8 in. (20 cm.)
*Geum* × *borisii*, 10 in. (25 cm.)
*Helenium* 'Wyndley', 24 in. (60 cm.)
*Helichrysum* 'Sulphur Light', 12 in. (30 cm.)
*Hemerocallis* 'Golden Chimes', or other dwarf variety,
    24–28 in. (60–70 cm.)
*Heuchera* 'Bressingham Blaze', 'Red Spangles', 'Scintil-
    lation', 16–24 in. (40–60 cm.)
*Hosta lancifolia*, 24 in. (60 cm.)
*Iris pallida* 'Variegata', 25 in. (70 cm.)
Kniphofia dwarf varieties, 28–36 in. (70–90 cm.)
*Liatris callilepis* 'Kobold', 20 in. (50 cm.)
*Liriope muscari*, 20 in. (50 cm.)
*Lythrum* 'Robert', 'Rose Queen', 28 in. (70 cm.)
Oenothera dwarf kinds, 8–16 in. (20–40 cm.)

*Origanum laevigatum*, 14 in. (35 cm.)
Phlox, varieties under 30 in. (75 cm.)
Platycodon, 16–24 in. (40–60 cm.)
*Polygonum carneum*, 20 in. (50 cm.)
*Potentilla* 'Gibson's Scarlet', 12 in. (30 cm.)
*Prunella* 'Loveliness', 10 in. (25 cm.)
*Ranunculus gramineus*, 12 in. (30 cm.)
*Rhazya orientalis*, 16 in. (40 cm.)
*Rudbeckia* 'Goldsturm', 24 in. (60 cm.)
*Salvia nemorosa* 'Superba', 44 in. (110 cm.)
*S. n.* dwarf varieties, 16–24 in. (40–60 cm.)
*Satureia montana*, 10 in. (25 cm.)
*Scabiosa graminifolia*, 10 in. (25 cm.)
   *S. caucasica*, 36 in. (90 cm.)
*Sedum spectabile* 18 in. (45 cm.) and 'Autumn Joy', 24 in. (60 cm.), 'Ruby Glow', 8 in. (20 cm.), 'Vera Johnson', 8 in. (20 cm.)
*Serratula shawii*, 10 in. (25 cm.)
*Sidalcea* 'Loveliness', 28 in. (70 cm.), 'Puck', 28 in. (70 cm.)
*Solidago* 'Golden Mosa', 24 in. (60 cm.), 'Golden Thumb', 10 in. (25 cm.)
*Stachys densiflora*, 18 in. (45 cm.)
   *S. spicata rosea*, 12 in. (30 cm.)
*Stokesia* 'Blue Star' and 'Wyoming', 16 in. (40 cm.)
Tradescantia in variety, 20 in. (50 cm.)
*Verbascum* 'Golden Bush', 20 in. (50 cm.)
*Veronica incana*, 12 in. (30 cm.)
   *V. petraea*, 6 in. (15 cm.)
   *V. spicata* 'Barcarolle', 'Minuet', 16 in. (40 cm.), 'Saraband', 20 in. (50 cm.)
   *V.* 'Shirley Blue', 8 in. (20 cm.)

# IV *A Selection of Taller Perennials which can generally be relied upon to need no staking*

*Approximate heights are given for established plants but may vary according to soil, climate and situation.*
*Those preferring some shade and/or moisture marked* S.M.

*Acanthus spinosus*, 44 in. (110 cm.)
*Achillea filipendulina* varieties, 40–60 in. (100–150 cm.)
*Aconitum bicolor*, 42 in. (105 cm.)
    *A.* 'Bressingham Spire', 32 in. (80 cm.)
    *A. carmichaelii* and *A. c.* 'Arendsii',' Newry Blue', 40–48 in. (100–120 cm.) S.M.
*Anemone hupehensis japonica* hybrids, 24–48 in. (60–120 cm.)
Agapanthus, 36–40 in. (90–100 cm.)
Anthericum, 40 in. (100 cm.)
*Artemisia lactiflora*, 48 in. (120 cm.)
*Aruncus dioicus* (syn. *A. sylvester*), 52 in. (130 cm.) S.M.
*Aster ericoides*, 36 in. (90 cm.)
    *A. frikartii*, 32 in. (80 cm.)
Astilbe, 20–60 in. (50–150 cm.) S.M.
*Campanula lactiflora* 'Prichard's Variety', 36 in. (90 cm.)
    *C. latifolia* vars., 48 in. (120 cm.)
    *C. latiloba* 'Percy Piper', 40 in. (100 cm.)
*Cautleya robusta*, 36–48 in. (90–120 cm.) S.M.
*Centaurea pulchra* 'Major', 40 in. (100 cm.)
    *C. ruthenica*, 48–60 in. (120–150 cm.)
*Cephalaria gigantea* (syn. *C. tatarica*), 52–64 in. (130–160 cm.)

77

*Chrysanthemum maximum* 'Wirral Supreme', 36 in. (90 cm.)

*Cichorium intybus* 'Roseum', 40 in. (100 cm.)

*Cimicifuga*, all spp., 36–60 in. (90–150 cm.) S.M.

*Crinum* × *powellii*, 36 in. (90 cm.)

Crocosmia, cultivars, 32–40 in. (80–100 cm.)

*Cynara scolymus glauca*, 72 in. (180 cm.)

Dictamnus, 36 in. (90 cm.)

Digitalis, 24–76 in. (60–190 cm.)

*Echinacea* Bressingham Hybrids, 36 in. (90 cm.)

*Echinops ritro*, 40 in. (100 cm.)

*Epilobium rosmarinifolium*, 48 in. (120 cm.)

*Eupatorium purpureum*, 60 in. (120–150 cm.)

*Euphorbia palustris*, 40 in. (100 cm.)

    *E. sikkimensis*, 48 in. (120 cm.)

*Filipendula elegantissima*, 36 in. (90 cm.) S.M.

*Galtonia candicans*, 40 in. (100 cm.)

*Gillenia trifoliata*, 36 in. (90 cm.) S.M.

Helenium, all except those over 44 in. (110 cm.) and *H.* 'Pumilum Magnificum'

*Helianthus* 'Loddon Gold', 48 in. (120 cm.)

*Heliopsis* 'Ballerina' and 'Golden Plume', 40 in. (100 cm.)

Hemerocallis, all varieties, 24–48 in. (60–120 cm.)

*Hosta* 'Honey Bells', 40 in. (100 cm.), 'Royal Standard', 40 in. (100 cm.) S.M.

    *H. rectifolia* ('Tallboy') 40–48 in. (100–120 cm.) S.M.

*Inula magnifica*, 64 in. (160 cm.)

*Iris sibirica*, 40–48 in. (100–120 cm.) S.M.

Kniphofia, most kinds, 36–60 in. (90–150 cm.)

*Ligularia* 'Gregynog Gold', 48 in. (120 cm.) S.M.

    *L. przewalskii* 'Sungold', 48 in. (120 cm.) S.M.

*Lunaria rediviva*, 40 in. (100 cm.)

*Lysimachia clethroides*, 48 in. (120 cm.)

    *L. ephemerum*, 48 in. (120 cm.)

Lythrum, 24–40 in. (60–100 cm.)
*Macleaya cordata*, 60–80 in. (150–200 cm.)
*Papaver orientalis* 'Goliath', 'Marcus Perry', 40 in. (100 cm.)
Phlox, most tall varieties, 18–48 in. (45–120 cm.)
Phormium, 32–72 in. (80–180 cm.)
*Polemonium foliosissimum*, 36–40 in. (90–100 cm.)
*Polygonum amplexicaule*, 48–56 in. (120–140 cm.)
    *P. bistorta* 'Superbum', 40 in. (100 cm.) S.M.
Rheum, 80–100 in. (200–250 cm.)
Rodgersia, 36–48 in. (90–120 cm.) S.M.
*Rudbeckia fulgida deamii*, 36 in. (90 cm.)
    *R.* 'Goldquelle', 40 in. (100 cm.)
*Salvia guaranitica* (syn. *S. ambigens*), 48 in. (120 cm.) S.M.
    *S. haematodes*, 48 in. (120 cm.)
    *S. nemorosa* 'Superba', 44 in. (110 cm.)
*Scabiosa caucasica*, 36 in. (90 cm.)
*Scrophularia aquatica* 'Variegata', 40 in. (100 cm.) S.M.
*Selinum tenuifolium*, 48 in. (120 cm.)
Sidalcea, most varieties, 32–48 in. (80–120 cm.)
*Strobilanthes atropurpurea*, 40 in. (100 cm.)
*Thalictrum aquilegifolium*, 40–48 in. (100–120 cm.)
    *T. angustifolium*, 56–64 in. (140–160 cm.)
    *T. flavum*, 48–60 in. (120–150 cm.)
    *T. roquebrunianum*, 60 in. (150 cm.) S.M.
Veratrum, 52–64 in. (130–160 cm.) S.M.
*Verbascum chaixii*, 64 in. (160 cm.)
    *V. thapsiforme*, 60 in. (150 cm.)
*Veronica virginica*, 64 in. (160 cm.)
Zantedeschia, 40–48 in. (100–120 cm.) S.M.

# V  *A Selection for Waterside Positions or Moist Soil*

*Those preferring some shade marked S. Wide variations in heights indicate different forms.*

*Alchemilla mollis*, 20 in. (50 cm.)
Aruncus, S., 28–60 in. (70–150 cm.)
Astilbe, S., 12–60 in. (30–150 cm.)
Astrantia, 20–36 in. (50–90 cm.)
Caltha, 10–20 in. (25–50 cm.)
Cautleya, S., 40 in. (100 cm.)
Cimicifuga, S., 40–64 in. (100–160 cm.)
Dierama, 36–56 in. (90–140 cm.)
Filipendula, most kinds, 20–60 in. (50–150 cm.)
*Gentiana asclepiadea*, S., 28 in. (70 cm.)
*Gillenia trifoliata*, S., 36 in. (90 cm.)
Hosta, 10–48 in. (25–120 cm.)
*Iris kaempferi, laevigata, pseudacorus, sibirica*, 28–40 in. (70–100 cm.)
Kirengeshoma, S., 36 in. (90 cm.)
Ligularia, 32–64 in. (80–160 cm.)
Lysichitum, 40 in. (100 cm.)
*Lysimachia punctata*, 40 in. (100 cm.)
Lythrum, 24–40 in. (60–100 cm.)
Mimulus, 8–24 in. (20–60 cm.)
Oenothera, 8–20 in. (20–50 cm.)
Peltiphyllum, 40 in. (100 cm.)
Podophyllum, 32 in. (80 cm.)
*Polygonum bistorta* 'Superbum', 40 in. (100 cm.)

*P. macrophyllum*, 20 in. (50 cm.)
*P. milletii*, 16 in. (40 cm.)
*P. sphaerostachyum*, 20 in. (50 cm.)
Primula, moisture-loving kinds, 12–36 in. (30–90 cm.)
*Ranunculus aconitifolius*, 24 in. (60 cm.)
Ranunculus, yellow-flowered kinds, 12–32 in. (30–80 cm.)
Rodgersia, S., 32–48 in. (80–120 cm.)
*Saxifraga fortunei*, S., 12 in. (30 cm.)
Schizostylis, 20–24 in. (50–60 cm.)
*Scrophularia aquatica* 'Variegata', 40 in. (100 cm.)
*Smilacina racemosa*, 36 in. (90 cm.)
Thalictrum, most kinds, 20–64 in. (50–160 cm.)
Tovara, 36–40 in. (90–100 cm.)
Tricyrtis, S., 20–28 in. (50–70 cm.)
Trollius, 12–36 in. (30–90 cm.)
Veratrum, S., 36–48 in. (90–120 cm.)
Zantedeschia, 40–48 in. (100–120 cm.)

# VI *A Selection for Hot, Dry Beds*

*Heights not given for prostrate or mat-forming kinds.*

Acaena in variety
Alyssum, 8 in. (20 cm.)
Andryala, 8 in. (20 cm.)
Anthyllis, 8 in. (20 cm.)
Arabis in variety
*Campanula garganica*
Cheiranthus, 8–20 in. (20–50 cm.)
*Crepis incana*, 16 in. (40 cm.)
Cytisus, up to 40 in. (100 cm.)
Erodium, 4–16 in. (10–40 cm.)
Euryops, 10 in. (25 cm.)
Genista, shrubby, up to 40 in. (100 cm.)
Geranium, dwarf kinds, 6–12 in. (15–30 cm.)
Gypsophila, prostrate kinds
Helichrysum, 4–10 in. (10–25 cm.)
Iberis, 4–10 in. (10–25 cm.)
Linum, 8–12 in. (20–30 cm.)
Pulsatilla, 8–12 in. (20–30 cm.)
Raoulia in variety
Santolina, 12–24 in. (30–60 cm.)
Saponaria in variety
Sedum, evergreen kinds
Sempervivum in variety
Thymus, most kinds
Zauschneria, 8–16 in. (20–40 cm.)

# VII  *A Selection for Growing between or near Paving on 'Walkabout' Beds in the Open*

*No heights given for prostrate or mat-forming kinds.*

Acaena in variety
Achillea in variety, 6–10 in. (15–20 cm.)
Ajuga in variety, 6–10 in. (15–20 cm.)
Antennaria in variety, 4–6 in. (10–15 cm.)
Arenaria in variety
Armeria in variety, 4–10 in. (10–25 cm.)
Campanula, prostrate or creeping kinds
Cotoneaster, prostrate kinds
Cotula in variety
Dianthus, close-growing kinds
Festuca (grass), 4–8 in. (10–20 cm.)
*Genista pilosa*
    *G. sagittalis*
Geranium, most dwarf kinds, 2–10 in. (5–25 cm.)
Hedera (Ivy), compact kinds
Hydrocotyle
*Hypsella reniformis* (syn. *H. longiflora*)
*Mazus pumilio*
    *M. reptans*
*Mentha requienii*
*Nierembergia repens* (syn. *N. rivularis*)
Raoulia in variety
*Saxifraga aizoon* forms, 4–10 in. (10–25 cm.)
Sedum, creeping kinds
Sempervivum
Thymus, creeping kinds
Veronica, prostrate kinds

# VIII  *A Selection for Ground Covering*

*For fairly dry shade*, D.S. *For less dry shade*, S. *All will
grow in more open positions.*

*Achillea* 'Moonshine', 20 in. (50 cm.)
*Ajuga reptans* in variety, S., 6–10 in. (15–25 cm.)
Alchemilla, S., 12–20 in. (30–50 cm.)
Anaphalis, S., 12–20 in. (30–50 cm.)
*Asarum europaeum*, D.S., 6 in. (15 cm.)
Bergenia, D.S., 12–20 in. (30–50 cm.)
*Brunnera macrophylla*, S., 16 in. (40 cm.)
*Campanula portenschlagiana*, D.S., 6–10 in. (15—25 cm.)
   *C. poscharskyana*, D.S., 6–10 in. (15–25 cm.)
Epimedium in variety, S., 8–16 in. (20–40 cm.)
*Geranium endressii* varieties, S., 16 in. (40 cm.)
   *G. macrorrhizum*, S., 12 in. (30 cm.)
   *G. phaeum*, D. S., 24 in. (60 cm.)
   *G. renardii*, 12 in. (30 cm.)
   *G. sanguineum* varieties, 12–16 in. (30–40 cm.)
   *G. sylvaticum*, D.S., 24 in. (60 cm.)
   Several named hybrids such as 'Claridge Druce', D.S.,
      12–24 in. (30–60 cm.)
× *Heucherella tiarelloides*, S., 12 in. (30 cm.)
Hosta (where not dry), S., 12–40 in. (30–100 cm.)
*Lamium garganicum*, S., 8 in. (20 cm.)
   *L. maculatum*, D.S., 8 in. (20 cm.)
*Liriope muscari*, 20 in. (50 cm.)
Mitella, D.S., 8 in. (20 cm.)
*Ophiopogon planiscapus*, D.S., 6 in. (15 cm.)

Pachysandra, D.S., 8 in. (20 cm.)
*Polygonum affine*, 8–12 in. (20–30 cm.)
Pulmonaria in variety, S., 6–16 in. (15–40 cm.)
*Reineckia carnea* (syn. *Liriope hyacinthiflora*), S., 12 in. (30 cm.)
*Ruta graveolens* 'Jackman's Blue', 24 in. (60 cm.)
*Saxifraga* × *urbium* (syn. *S. umbrosa*) forms, D.S., 6–10 in. (15–23 cm.)
Santolina, 10–20 in. (25–50 cm.)
*Satureia montana*, 10 in. (25 cm.)
*Sedum spurium* 'Green Mantle'
*Stachys olympica* (syn. *S. lanata*), 20 in. (50 cm.)
*Symphytum grandiflorum*, D.S., 8 in. (20 cm.)
*Tellima grandiflora*, D.S., 20 in. (50 cm.)
Tiarella (not dry), S., 10 in. (25 cm.)
Vinca, all forms, D.S., 4–10 in. (10–25 cm.)
*Waldsteinia ternata*, D.S., 6 in. (15 cm.)


ORNAMENTAL GRASSES FOR GROUND COVER
*Acorus gramineus*, 6 in. (15 cm.)
*Arrhenatherum elatius bulbosum variegatum*, 10 in. (25 cm.)
*Avena candida*, 24 in. (60 cm.)
*Carex morrowii*, 10 in. (25 cm.)
*Dactylis glomerata variegata*, 6 in. (15 cm.)
Festuca, 4–12 in. (10–30 cm.)
*Holcus mollis variegatus*, 10 in. (25 cm.)
Luzula, 10–20 in. (25–50 cm.)
*Molinia caerulea*, 20–24 in. (50–60 cm.)
*Phalaris arundinacea* 'Picta' (invasive), 24–28 in. (60–70 cm.)

## IX  *A Selection of Ornamental Grasses, mainly for Sunny Positions*

*Andropleion scoparius*, 30 in. (75 cm.)
*Avena candida*, 36 in. (90 cm.)
*Bouteloua gracilis*, 12 in. (30 cm.)
*Calamagrostis epigios hortorum*, 48 in. (120 cm.)
Carex, 6–16 in. (15–40 cm.)
*Cortaderia selloana* (syn. *C. argentea*) (Pampas Grass),
    48–80 in. (120–200 cm.)
*Festuca glauca*, 8 in. (20 cm.)
Hakonechloa, 10 in. (15 cm.)
*Helictotrichon sempervirens* (syn. *Avena candida*), 40 in.
    (100 cm.)
*Lasiogrostis splendens*, 52 in. (130 cm.)
*Luzula nivea*, 18 in. (45 cm.)
*Luzula pilosa*, 12 in. (30 cm.)
Miscanthus, 40–100 in. (100–250 cm.)
Molinia, 16–48 in. (40–120 cm.)
*Panicum miliaceum*, 40 in. (100 cm.)
    *P. virgatum*, 40 in. (100 cm.)
Pennisetum, 16–40 in. (40–100 cm.)
Sesleria, 12–32 in. (30–80 cm.)
Stipa, 36–60 in. (90–150 cm.)

# General Index

———❈———

*Aster Nova Belgii see* Michael-
   mas daisy
Achillea, 57
*Alchemilla mollis*, 62
Andromeda, 42
Astilbe, 59–60, 63
Aubrieta, 22
Azalea, 42

Bergenia, 51
Bressingham, 21, 52
Bricks, 37, 43

Calluna, 42
Campanula, 19, 57
Cimicifuga, 57
*Compositae*, 63
Compost, 59–60
Concrete blocks, 37
Conifers, 40–42

Daphne, 42
Dell, The, 23
Delphinium, 12, 16, 19, 22,
   41, 61
*Dictionary of Gardening*, 12
Drainage, 27, 44–45, 59

Drought, 57–59

Epimedium, 51
*Erica carnea*, 41

Fertilizer, 59–60

Gauntlett, 15
Geranium, 62–63
Geum, 63
Golden rod *see* Solidago
Gravetye, 14

Heathers, 37, 40–42
Hedges, 49–50
Helenium, 30, 63
Helianthus, 47, 63
Herbaceous borders, 12–20,
   47–50
Heuchera, 12, 60, 63
Hosta, 60
Humus, 59

Iris, 16

Jekyll, Gertrude, 13–15

Kniphofia, 12, 30, 32

Lawns, 17, 21, 26, 50, 52

Macleaya, 63
Michaelmas daisy, 16, 30, 32, 63
Midget island beds, 40–41
Miller, Phillip, 12
Moisture-loving plants, 43–45, 59
Monarda, 63
Mulching, 59–61, 63

Peat, 27, 35, 41, 43, 59–61
Peat blocks, 37–38, 42–44
Peony, 16
Perennial sunflower *see* Helianthus
*Perennials for Trouble-Free Gardening*, 55
Phlox, 12, 16, 60
Physostegia, 63
Planning, 26–33, 56
Planting, 34–35, 57
Polygala, 42
Polythene sheeting, 44
Pools, 40, 43–44
Portugal laurels, 51
Potentilla, 62
Primula, 51
Pulmonaria, 51

Quality, 36

Raised beds, 37–39, 41
Ranunculus, 59
Rejuvenating, 64
Replanting, 62–64
Robinson, William, 13–15
Rocks, 37, 44
Royal Horticultural Society, 15
Rudbeckia, 57

Sand, 27, 35
Saxifrage, 22
Shakespeare, 11
Sink garden, 37
Soil conditions, 24, 34–35
Soil exhaustion, 62–63
Solidago, 47
Spenser, 11
Staking, 19–20, 61–62, 64
Stones, 37, 43

Trollius, 59
Trough garden, 37

Veitch, 15

'Walkabout' island beds, 39–40
Walls, 37–39, 42–43, 49, 53
Ware, Thomas, 15
Weeds, 27, 48, 56, 59

# Index of Selected Lists

Acaena, 82, 83
*Acanthus spinosus*, 77
Achillea, 71, 83
   *A. filipendulina*, 77
   *A.* 'Moonshine', 74, 84
*Aconitum, bicolor*, 77
   *A.* 'Bressingham Spire', 77
   *A. carmichaelii*, 77
   *A.c.* 'Arendsii', 77
   *A.c.* 'Newry Blue', 77
*Acorus gramineus*, 69, 85
*Adiantum venustum*, 69
Adonis, 69
   *A. amurensis* 'Pleniflora', 74
   *A.* 'Fukujukai', 74
*Aethionema* 'Warley Rose', 71
Agapanthus, 77
Ajuga, 83
   *A. pyramidalis*, 69
   *A. reptans*, 84
Alchemilla, 84
   *A. mollis*, 80
Allium, 71
Alyssum, 71, 82
Anaphalis, 84
Andromeda, 69
*Andropleion scoparius*, 86

Androsace, 71
Andryala, 82
*Anemone* 'Bressingham Glow', 74
   *A.* 'September Charm', 74
   *A. hupehensis japonica*, 77
Antennaria, 83
*Anthemis rudolphiana*, 74
   *A. sancti-johannis*, 74
Anthericum, 77
Anthyllis, 82
Aquilegia, 71
Arabis, 71, 82
Arenaria, 83
Armeria, 71, 83
   *A.* 'Bees Ruby', 74
   *A.* 'Dusseldorf', 74
*Arrhenatherum elatus bulbosum variegatum*, 85
*Artemisia lactiflora*, 77
Aruncus, 80
   *A. dioicus* (Sylvester), 77
*Asarum europaeum*, 84
Asperula, 71
Asplenium, 69
Aster, dwarf hybrids:
   'Jenny', 74;

'Lady in Blue', 74
'Little Pink Beauty', 74
*Aster ericoides*, 77
  *A. frikartii*, 74, 77
  *A.* 'Jubilee', 74
  *A.* 'Violet Queen', 74
  *A. novi-belgii* 'Carnival', 74
  *A. n-b.* 'Royal Ruby', 74
  *A.n-b.* 'Royal Violet', 74
  *A. thomsonii* 'Nanus', 74
Astilbe, 69, 77, 80
Astrantia, 80
Aubrieta, 71
*Avena candida*, 86

*Bouteloua gracilis*, 86

*Calamagrostis epigios hortorum*, 86
Caltha, 80
  *C. leptosepala*, 69
*Campanula alliariifolia* 'Ivory Bells', 74
  *C. carpatica*, 71
  *C.c.* 'Blue Moonlight', 74
  *C.c.* 'Bressingham White', 74
  *C.c.* 'Isobel', 74
  *C. garganica*, 71, 82
  *C. glomerata* 'Nana Alba', 74
  *C. lactiflora* 'Prichard's Variety', 77
  *C. latifolia*, 77
  *C. latiloba* 'Percy Piper', 77
  *C.* 'Molly Pinsent', 74
  *C. muralis*, 71
  *C. portenschlagiana*, 71, 74, 84

*C. poscharskyana*, 84
*C. stansfieldii*, 71
*C.* 'Stella', 71
*C. turbinata*, 71
*Carduncellus rhaponticoides*, 71
Carex, 86
  *C. morrowii*, 85
Cautleya, 80
  *C. robusta*, 77
*Centaurea hypoleuca*, 74
  *C. pulchra* 'Major', 77
  *C. ruthenica*, 77
*Cephalaria gigantea*, 77
Cheiranthus, 71, 82
Chiastophyllum, 69, 75
  *C. oppositifolium*, 71
*Chrysanthemum maximum* 'Wirral Supreme', 77
*Chrysogonum virginianum*, 69, 75
*Cichorium intybus* 'Roseum', 78
*Cimicifuga*, 78, 80
*Clematis integrifolia* 'Hendersonii', 75
Codonopsis, 69
*Coreopsis verticillata*, 75
*Cortaderia selloana*, 86
Cortusa, 69
Cotoneaster, 83
Cotula, 83
*Crepis incana*, 71, 75, 82
*Crinum* × *powellii*, 78
Crocosmia masonorum, 75, 78
*Cyananthus lobatus*, 69
Cyclamen, 69
*Cynara scolymus glauca*, 78
Cytisus, 82

*Dactylis glomerata variegata*, 85
*Deinanthe coerulea*, 69
Dianthus, 72, 83
   *D.* 'Mrs Pilkington', 75
*Dicentra* 'Adrian Bloom', 75
   *D. spectabilis*, 75
Dictamnus, 78
Dierama, 80
Digitalis, 78
Disporum, 69
Dodecatheon, 69
*Doronicum* 'Spring Beauty', 75
Draba, 72

*Echinacea* Bressingham Hybrids, 78
*Echinops ritro*, 78
*Epilobium rosmarinifolium*, 78
Epimedium, 84
   *E.* × *youngianum* 'Niveum', 69
*Erigeron* dwarf vars., 75
Erinus, 72
Erodium, 72, 82
*Eryngium bourgatii*, 75
*Erythronium californicum*, 69
*Eupatorium purpureum*, 78
*Euphorbia palustris*, 78
   *E. polychroma*, 75
   *E. sikkimensis*, 78
Euryops, 82

Festuca, 83, 85
   *F. glauca*, 86
Filipendula, 80
   *F. elegantissima*, 78
   *F. hexapetala* 'Plena', 75

*Galtonia candicans*, 78
Genista, 82
   *G. pilosa*, 83
   *G. sagittalis*, 83
Gentiana, 72
   *G. asclepiadea*, 69, 80
   *G. septemfida*, 75
Geranium, 72, 82, 83
   *G.* 'Claridge Druce', 84
   *G. endressii*, 84
   *G.* 'Johnson's Blue', 75
   *G. macrorrhizum*, 84
   *G. phaeum*, 84
   *G. renardii*, 75, 84
   *G. sanguineum*, 84
   *G. subcaulescens*, 75
   *G. sylvaticum*, 84
*Gillenia trifoliata*, 78, 80
Globularia, 72
Gypsophila, 72, 82

Haberlea, 70
*Hacquetia epipactis*, 70
Hedera, 83
Helenium, 78
   *H.* 'Pumilum Magnificum', 78
   *H.* 'Wyndley', 75
Helianthemum, 72
*Helianthus* 'Loddon Gold', 78
Helichrysum, 72, 82
   *H.* 'Sulphur Light', 75
*Helictotrichon sempervirens*, 86
*Heliopsis* 'Ballerina', 78
   *H.* 'Golden Plume', 78
Helleborus, 70
Hemerocallis, 78

*H.* 'Golden Chimes', 75
Hepatica, 70
Heuchera 'Bressingham Blaze', 75
   *H.* 'Red Spangles', 75
   *H.* 'Scintillation', 75
*Heucherella tiarelloides*, 84
*Holcus mollis variegata*, 85
Hosta, 70, 80, 84
   *H.* 'Honey Bells', 78
   *H. lancifolia*, 75
   *H. rectifolia*, 78
   *H.* 'Royal Standard', 78
Hydrocotyle, 83
Hypericum, 72
*Hypsella reniformis*, 83

Iberis, 72, 82
*Incarvillea grandiflora*, 70
*Inula magnifica*, 78
*Iris kaempferi*, 80
   *I. laevigata*, 80
   *I. pallida* 'Variegata', 75

Kirengeshoma, 80
Kniphofia, 75, 78

*Lamium garganicum*, 84
   *L. maculatum*, 84
*Lasiogrostis splendens*, 86
Lewisia, 72
*Liatris callilepis* 'Kobold', 75
Ligularia, 80
   *L.* 'Gregynog Gold', 78
   *L. przewalskii* 'Sungold', 78
Limonium, 72
Linum, 72, 82

*Liriope muscari*, 75, 84
*Lunaria rediviva*, 78
Luzula, 85
   *L. nivea*, 86
   *L. pilosa*, 86
*Lysimachia clethroides*, 78
   *L. ephemerum*, 78
   *L. punctata*, 80
Lysichitum, 80
Lythrum, 78, 80
   *L.* 'Robert', 75
   *L.* 'Rose Queen', 75

*Macleaya cordata*, 78
*Mazus pumilio*, 83
   *M. reptans*, 83
*Meconopsis quintuplinervia*, 70
*Mentha requinii*, 70, 83
Micromeria, 72
Mimulus, 80
Miscanthus, 86
Mitella, 84
Molinia, 86
   *M. caerulea*, 85
Moltkia, 72
Morisia, 72
*Myosotis rupicola*, 72

*Nierembergia repens*, 83

Oenothera, 75, 80
Omphalodes, 70
Ophiopogon, 70
   *O. planiscapus*, 84
Orchis, 70
Origanum, 72
   *O. laevigatum*, 76

Ourisia, 70

Pachysandra, 84
*Panicum miliaceum*, 86
 *P. virgatum*, 86
*Papaver orientalis* 'Goliath', 79
 *P.o.* 'Marcus Perry', 79
Parahebe, 72
Peltiphyllum, 80
Pennisetum, 86
Penstemon, 72
*Phalaris arundinacea* 'Picta', 85
Phlox, 76, 79
 *P. adsurgens*, 70
 *P. douglasii*, 72
 *P. pilosa*, 70
 *P. subulata*, 72
Phormium, 79
Platycodon, 70, 76
Podophyllum, 80
*Polemonium foliosissimum*, 79
*Polygala chamaebuxus*, 70
 *P. vayredae*, 70
*Polygonatum hookeri*, 70
*Polygonum affine*, 85
 *P. amplexicaule*, 79
 *P. bistorta* 'Superbum', 79, 80
 *P. carneum*, 76
 *P. macrophyllum*, 70, 81
 *P. milletii*, 70, 81
 *P. sphaerostachyum*, 81
 *P. vaccinifolium*, 72
Potentilla, 72
 *P.* 'Gibson's Scarlet', 76
Primula, 70, 81

*Prunella* 'Loveliness', 76
Pulmonaria, 85
Pulsatilla, 82

Ramonda, 70, 72
Ranunculus, 81
 *R. aconitifolius*, 81
 *R. gramineus*, 76
Raoulia, 72, 82, 83
*Reineckia carnea*, 85
*Rhazya orientalis*, 76
Rheum, 79
Rhododendron, 70
Rodgersia, 79, 81
*Rudbeckia fulgida deamii*, 79
 *R.* 'Goldquelle', 79
 *R.* 'Goldsturm', 76
*Ruta graveolens* 'Jackman's Blue', 85

*Salvia* dwarf var., 76
 *S. guaranitica*, 79
 *S. haematodes*, 79
 *S. nemerosa* 'Superba', 76, 79
Santolina, 82, 85
Saponaria, 72, 82
*Satureia montana*, 76, 85
Saxifraga, 70
 *S. aizoon*, 72, 83
 *S. fortunei*, 81
 *S.* × *urbium*, 85
*Scabiosa caucasica*, 76, 79
 *S. graminifolia*, 76
Schizostylis, 81
*Scrophularia aquatica* 'Variegata', 79, 81

Sedum, 72, 82, 83
    *S.* 'Autumn Joy', 76
    *S.* 'Ruby Glow', 76
    *S. spectabile*, 76
    *S. spurium* 'Green Mantle', 85
    *S.* 'Vera Johnson', 76
*Selinum tenuifolium*, 79
Sempervivum, 72, 82, 83
*Serratula shawii*, 76
Sesleria, 86
Sidalcea, 79
    *S.* 'Loveliness', 76
    *S.* 'Puck', 76
Silene, 73
*Smilacina racemosa*, 81
Soldanella, 70
*Solidago* 'Golden Mosa', 76
    *S.* 'Golden Thumb', 76
*Stachys densiflora*, 76
    *S. olympica*, 85
    *S. spicata rosea*, 76
Stipa, 86
*Stokesia* 'Blue Star', 76
    *S.* 'Wyoming', 76
*Strobilanthes atropurpurea*, 79
*Symphytum grandiflorum*, 85
Synthyris, 70

*Tellima grandiflora*, 85
Thalictrum, 70, 81

*T. angustifolium*, 79
*T. aquilegifolium*, 79
*T. flavum*, 79
*T. rocquebrunianum*, 79
Thymus, 73, 82, 83
Tiarella, 70, 85
Tovara, 81
Tradescantia, 76
Tricyrtis, 81
Trillium, 70
Trollius, 81
Tunica, 73

Veratrum, 79, 81
*Verbascum chaixii*, 79
    *V.* 'Golden Bush', 76
    *V. thapsiforme*, 79
Veronica, 73, 83
    *V. incana*, 76
    *V. petraea*, 76
    *V. virginica*, 79
    *V. spicata* 'Barcarolle', 76
    *V.s.* 'Minuet', 76
    *V.s.* 'Saraband', 76
    *V.s.* 'Shirley Blue', 76
Vinca, 85

*Waldsteinia ternata*, 85

Zantedeschia, 79, 81
Zauschneria, 73, 82